LIFE ON MARS

THE OFFICIAL COMPANION : VOLUME TWO

LIFE | ON
MARS

THE OFFICIAL COMPANION : VOLUME TWO

WRITTEN BY GUY ADAMS
DESIGNED BY LEE THOMPSON

POCKET
BOOKS

London • New York • Sydney • Toronto

First Published in Great Britain by Pocket Books, 2007
An imprint of Simon and Schuster UK
A CBS Company

A CIP catalogue record for this book is available from the British Library.

1 3 5 7 9 10 8 6 4 2
ISBN-10: 1-84739-039-0
ISBN-13: 978-1-84739-039-4

Writer: Guy Adams
Designer: Lee Thompson
Commissioning Editor: Sally Partington

Simon & Schuster UK Ltd.
Africa House
64-78 Kingsway
London WC2B 6AH

www.simonsays.co.uk
www.kudosfilmandtv.com
www.bbc.co.uk/lifeonmars

Printed and bound in Germany by Mohn Media.

CONTENTS

FOREWORD
CLAIRE PARKER

No one thought *Life On Mars* would work. The first draft gathered dust on the shelf for years, overlooked by commissioners. And every time I mentioned the concept to friends they gave me a pitying look and prepared to nurse me through a flop. Those of us closest to the series always believed in it and hoped that eventually, others would too. But, even for the faithful, what happened next was beyond our expectations.

Seven years after the idea was first born during a brainstorm in windswept Blackpool, 7.4 million viewers tuned into the finale. For that brief moment it was as if everyone in the country was gripped by Sam Tyler's destiny. Newspaper columns brimmed with analysis of why Gene Hunt was so popular, internet message boards buzzed with theories about the show's secret meaning and even policemen at the Old Bailey whose heyday was in 1973 indulged in nostalgic chats about Gene Hunt's robust methods.

I wasn't there quite from the beginning when Matthew Graham, Ashley Pharoah and Tony Jordan wrote the words '70s cop – Ford Granada' on a flip chart and *Life On Mars* was born. But the series has been a huge part of my life – and the lives of many of us – for several years. I've watched it cast a spell over anyone who became involved and there was a fantastic creative energy as the series started to come together. Dean Andrews, who plays Ray, echoed all our feelings when he said to me: 'You give a lot to every show you work on. But it's rare to give part of your soul.'

Everyone who watched *Life On Mars* has their favourite episode and favourite line. But from my position behind the camera, my memories are of an intensely creative collaboration. It starts with the writing. Matthew, Ashley and Tony had all written successful series, but this was the first time that they had come together to co-create. The confidence and joy that is so evident when they are in a room together – particularly if there is alcohol involved – shines through in the scripts (where there is often, by strange coincidence, alcohol involved).

After they set the tone, it was easy to persuade other top writers to join them. And good writing attracts good directors. Led by Bharat Nalluri on the first series and SJ Clarkson on the second, the directors expended endless energy, enthusiasm and originality in bringing the show to life.

On screen, John Simm was simply dream casting for the role of Sam Tyler

and I was overjoyed when he loved the script. He was our first choice and, even with all the anticipation of what he would bring to the role, he exceeded our hopes. But the real surprise was seeing the chemistry emerge, and then continue to build, between him and Philip Glenister. Everyone watched in delight as Philip slipped on his white shoes and camel coat and started to inhabit a character that had leapt off the page, but sparkled on the monitors in the studio. Even so, we had no idea that Gene Hunt would become such a cult hit when the series was finally broadcast.

The success of series one with the critics and viewers meant the atmosphere when we started shooting the second series had changed dramatically. Instead of blank looks from passers-by baffled by our retro cast crowded round a Ford Cortina, we were surrounded by excited fans hoping to snap pictures of Sam, Gene and Annie on their mobile phone cameras. Now aware of the reaction to the first series which had built up excitement and trust from the viewers, we put huge pressure on ourselves to ensure we didn't disappoint. We were determined to make the second series even better and bring it to a climax that not only satisfied, but exceeded, everyone's expectations.

And so we finally reached the end of the second series. The last scene we shot only involved John so it could have been a lonely and anticlimactic end to thousands of hours of filming. But instead, the rest of the cast came back to watch the final take and there was a celebratory as well as an emotional atmosphere on set. And as Sam hung up his leather jacket and left his bedroom for the last time, SJ Clarkson called wrap on *Life On Mars*.

But as Gene himself would say: 'No need to come over all Dorothy…'

Claire Parker
September 2007

INTRODUCTION
CAMERON ROACH

Cameron and Claire finally out of flares at the Monte Carlo TV festival

The 'second album' syndrome is a well known hazard of the music business, just as second novel syndrome afflicts bestselling debut authors. Could the same thing happen to the phenomenon that is (was) *Life On Mars*? Coming on board as producer for the second series was a daunting prospect. Just as I signed on the dotted line the first series was fast becoming a runaway success: within weeks of being on air the show had spawned not only a terrifically popular fan site but seemingly acres of press – it felt as though water-cooler TV had been reinvented. By the end of series one the audience had incredibly high expectations of where *Life On Mars* might go, so it was inevitable that I felt a terrific responsibility.

Before being formally offered the job, I'd been summoned to meet Matthew Graham. Having watched the pilot episode and been overwhelmed by its brilliance, in my mind Matthew was already a legend. I was imagining a Gene Hunt character, and here I was, a Sam Tyler misfit about to step on to his hallowed turf. Rather appropriately, we met in a pub on Exmouth Market, not unlike the Railway Arms. When Matthew offered me a drink I decided to go for a pint of ale (I thought ordering a bottle of Peroni might well immediately signal my unsuitability for the project) and I was ready to inhale twenty Benson and Hedges if need be to impress this demi-god. Thankfully Matthew is an incredibly generous and down-to-earth person, and was keen to hear my views on the series and what I thought about each of the characters. By our third pint, having bonded over Sam, Gene and Annie, a mutual admiration for the Ford Cortina and a shared knowledge of the Bath and West Show, Matthew, in agreement with Claire Parker and Jane Featherstone of Kudos, invited me to join them.

From my first meetings with the creative team it was agreed that the second series should feel like a continuation of the first. This was a show that needed no reinvention; it was clear that the audience wanted 'more of the same'. Yet that was also our biggest challenge, since 'more of the same' meant that viewers expected to be constantly surprised and amazed by Sam's world. We knew that we would have to work hard to ensure that the levels of

mystery within Sam's journey were maintained, while still telling compelling crime stories with a flourish of humour and entertainment.

I think we all felt that the second series could afford to be slightly darker in tone, and that issues could be examined in further detail without the series beginning to feel too 'heavy'; so we began to plan for episodes in which we'd go deep into the Irish and Asian communities of 1973 Manchester, and also take a trip into pampas-grass-ridden suburbia. Maintaining the 1973 look through effective location management and design was a constant challenge, but the team behind *Life On Mars* invariably went the extra mile to make sure that the settings were authentic. The fact that every member of the production team knew how special this project was spurred them on.

At the same time as preserving the key elements of series one, we needed to allow for character development in our core cast. So although Sam still felt as much out of place as before, it was inevitable that because of the time he'd spent in 1973 he would begin to form deeper bonds with the members of A division. Ashley drew on this when he wrote the brilliant scene in episode four in which we see Sam giving girlfriend advice to Chris, and of course there was the ongoing Annie-Sam relationship which we hoped would keep fans in suspense throughout the series. That's not to say that conflict wouldn't remain a constant in the Sam-Gene dynamic. We were all aware that this feuding partnership, as long as we maintained it effectively, could go down as one of TV's most memorable double acts.

As a producer, it's a luxury to know that the series you are working on has a definite 'end' – and while we debated at length exactly how that end should play out, even into the edit suite, we felt strongly as an editorial team that we had done justice to Sam's journey. It was still a relief when the majority of the audience voiced their satisfaction as episode eight transmitted.

One of the most complex and difficult sequences was the team's final train journey and the subsequent shoot-out scenario. Planning for this involved me, director SJ Clarkson and Marcus Wilson (co-producer, and a strategic mastermind) trudging along miles of railway track and spending unhealthy periods of time in dark tunnels with flashlights (and, on one rather unproductive outing, without a flashlight!) SJ and director of photography Tim Palmer planned this sequence meticulously, which resulted in a visual tour de force and a magnificent launch pad to propel Sam back into 2007.

There was a very strange atmosphere on set the day we shot Sam's modern office sequence. John Simm commented that it felt odd not to be in his leather jacket and no longer occupying the seventies world. It was an emotional moment too for both SJ and Claire as we shot these scenes which marked an end to the *Life On Mars* journey. That feeling of sadness and dislocation was captured on film in the sense of unease which comes through clearly on screen. It's an immensely effective sequence and one we were extremely proud of.

For me, the second series of *Life On Mars* was an unforgettable experience; tough at times but ultimately hugely rewarding. Let's face it, spending a year on a show involving fast cars, guns and casinos was never going to be too much of a hardship!

Cameron Roach
September 2007

Cameron, Claire, Phil, Matthew & John just after we wrapped on the shoot

Back in the nick of time.

BBC 1 *COLOUR*

Life On Mars.
The drama returns
Tuesday 13th February

LOST AND FOUND:
LAST TIME IN 1973...

Thompson had banged on the top of the black and white television so often he was beginning to think there was more pleasure in the violence of it than in watching the grainy pictures it sometimes had the decency to show.

'There we go,' said a familiar, comforting voice from the speaker which made everything sound as though it was recorded on a submarine. 'Tiny Clanger's found the Music Boat.'

'Not exactly *Desperate Housewives*, but it'll do…' thought Thompson as he slumped into a beaten old armchair and sipped at a gin and tonic so strong that only Richard Burton wouldn't raise an eyebrow at him drinking it in the middle of the afternoon.

He watched the jerky pink Clangers navigate their cold and inhospitable world with a smile. They whistled and chomped on blue string pudding as his eyes began to droop.

'Oh look!' the narrator said, louder than before. 'Thompson's fallen asleep in his chair!'

Thompson twitched and stared at the screen. Had he really heard that? There was nothing on the static-filled landscape: Tiny Clanger must have sailed away.

'He thinks he's imagining the voices,' the narrator continued in a conspiratorial tone. 'But he and Adams imagine a lot of things since the accident, don't they?'

The voice didn't seem to be coming from the TV any more; it was louder … clearer. He caught a glimpse of something from the corner of his eye… Something *pink*.

On the television he could see himself sat on an InterCity train, tapping away at his laptop; his old life, before 1973…

'They thought it was a simple job,' the narrator was explaining. 'A book about the series *Life On Mars*.' On the screen he saw Adams, his friend and the writer of the book they had been working on, dozing peacefully, unaware of the danger that lay further down the track. Suddenly the picture tumbled, the train they were sat on derailing, the air filling with hurled baggage and abandoned newspapers. '*Boom! Crash! Bang!*' said the narrator. 'And they wake up inside the very programme they had been writing about. How very strange!'

Something distracted Thompson from the screen. There! He distinctly saw *something* run past the foot of the bed. A noise … *whistling*?

'And now they're stuck,' the voice continued. 'Wearing bad clothes in a dark brown seventies world.'

Something grabbed his foot; something small, pink and … knitted?

'The Clangers want to tell him how silly he is! Sitting around drinking wobble soup in the middle of the day when he should be out there making the best of it.'

There was a pain in his ankle as something sharp – a needle maybe? – jabbed into him.

'Ow! You stupid pink…' He didn't finish his sentence as the small pan that Major Clanger had appropriated from the dirty sink whacked into the back of his head.

'Major Clanger won't stand for that! He thinks Thompson should stop sitting around whinging in his dump of a flat and start being useful.'

Thompson felt both feet being yanked as he was pulled from the chair and onto the floor. Struggling to get his wind back he saw a pair of Clangers tugging on the cuffs of his flared trousers.

'Small Clanger and Tiny Clanger want to play with him!' the narrator continued. 'I hope they don't break him…'

Major Clanger whistled orders to his small charges from the arm of the easy-chair Thompson had so recently left.

'Major Clanger wants to know if Thompson tastes better than soup.' There was an edge to the narrator's voice now, it seemed sharper, nastier than he remembered from childhood. 'Maybe they should boil him up and find out!' it concluded with some relish. 'Thompson's beginning to panic. It seems ridiculous to be scared of such little pink fellows but, try as he might, he just can't seem to move.'

This was true, he was utterly still as Mother Clanger climbed onto his chest and began to sing while waving her little tankard.

There was a banging at the door, which Thompson hoped fervently was Adams come to rescue him from his hungry pink attackers. It grew progressively louder until the door burst open and Adams fell in to the room. He swore and kicked at the doorframe. 'Bloody thing was stuck again.' He looked at his friend, lying, for no earthly reason that he could tell, in the middle of the floor. 'What are you doing down there?'

Thompson looked around to make sure all of the Clangers had vanished. Then he gave it a couple of seconds to allow the narrator to describe him checking … but it seemed he'd vanished too.

'Nothing…' He got up and brushed himself down, 'Just, y'know … erm … *nothing*. Let's go out.'

Adams shrugged, 'Okay. We've had a call anyway, a juicy bit of murder!'

They hurried out of the flat together, Adams smiling quizzically at his friend's peculiar ways. Neither of them thought to turn off the television.

'Wasteful buggers,' the narrator said, and promptly turned it off himself.

A LEAP OF FAITH
Matthew Graham looks back

Television is a collaborative art like no other, everyone from director to electrician coming together to get a story onto the screen and into the viewer's consciousness.

Still, that story has to start somewhere and before it's dragged – maybe kicking and screaming – through a battlefield of meetings, edits, locations and camera work, it is a fragile thing inside someone's head, waiting to be fleshed out. Matthew Graham, co-creator, writer and executive producer, is the starting point for much of *Life On Mars*. In his often delightfully chaotic imagination, *Camberwick Green* exists side-by-side with vicious casino bosses and illusory police detectives. A story that he had every sensible expectation of never getting to tell – that of a comatose policeman in a fever dream – had been realized and enjoyed by millions. Not only had it been commissioned in the first place, but such was the commitment of the BBC that they bought a second series before

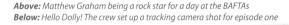

Above: Matthew Graham being a rock star for a day at the BAFTAs
Below: Hello Dolly! The crew set up a tracking camera shot for episode one

they had begun to screen the first: a decision made on the final day of filming the first series.

'It took about twenty seconds to stop cheering and start worrying,' he admits. 'It was actually all rather stifled. The BBC told Jane, Claire [Featherstone and Parker, Matthew's fellow executive producers] and myself but we decided not to tell the cast that night. They were all shattered from five months' filming and we thought it might just fill them with dread if that very night they had to contemplate doing it all over again. I remember drinking heavily with Dean Andrews [DC Ray Carling] at the wrap party and he was so anxious about when the BBC might make a decision to go again. I told him as delicately as I could that he wasn't to lose too much sleep on that score. He pretty much got the message. Personally I was so impressed by the BBC's willingness to greenlight a second series before they even saw how the first performed. We knew we had to prove to them that they'd made the right leap.'

Prove it they certainly did, although with the runaway success

> **"I even remember at one point suggesting that Sam should hallucinate a pig being butchered at odd moments during the show – a metaphor for the death of Gene!"**

of the first series came a further problem: everyone was under pressure to make series two match that success.

'Series one had no expectations: it just snuck in under the wire. There was no way we could surprise an audience to that extent again. Everyone had their own theories about what should happen to Sam and Gene. I tried to blot them out. I had an ending in mind. We had all agreed pretty much what was going to happen; it was just a case of getting our heads down and getting the story to its conclusion. You have to be guided by your own instincts and not those of the public, even if they're ardent fans. After all, it was our instincts that got series one into the nation's consciousness in the first place!'

As the man charged with writing the first episode of the new series the onus was squarely on Matthew to meet that expectation head on.

'It was essential when starting series two to remind the audience as subtly as possible of all the characters and states of play – plus of course what is at stake. That meant opening with the coma and then giving Gene a big, brash, door-kicking entrance. Crash into The Sweet or T-Rex or some-such; cut to the car and Bob's your uncle. I liked delaying Annie's arrival. The coy way she tugs on the police cordon rope whilst Sam is holding it…'

SHOOTING SCRIPT EXTRACT - Episode 1

INT. SAM'S FLAT - DAY 1/1 0830

Wooden TV - programme flashes on and off; "Z-Cars" or something similar. Cops with bad cars after villains with bad hair. TRACK AROUND the flat (airier and more book-lined than before) as hospital sounds drift in like smoke - heart monitor ping, rise and fall of the respirator.

Settle upon SAM TYLER on his back in bed, like a corpse.

Far away, in another room, music - Kaiser Chiefs "I Predict A Riot". SAM'S eyes flicker open. Light fills the room - supernaturally intense. He glances woozily at the 1973 calendar on his wall (May). For a moment it flashes into a hospital poster on MRSA.

Footsteps. A FIGURE emerges from the light. Moves around SAM'S bed, whistling softly to himself - "Bring Me Sunshine" from The Morecambe And Wise Show. But there is nothing carefree about this FIGURE - there is an easygoing malevolence in his presence. SAM tries to speak but can't - is this a dream? An arm reaches over SAM to adjust the life support array. SAM jolts in his bed. Struck by a pain in his body.

SAM: Help me. Help me...

An insistent banging starts from seemingly far away. SAM is confused and in pain and it's getting worse. And the banging is getting louder and more demanding and then - SAM jolts out of sleep as his door is kicked open. We're back in the "real" world. DCI GENE HUNT - great smell of Brut mangod, glaring down at him.

There was also a notable increase in the more surreal elements of the narrative, those moments when reality intrudes on Sam Tyler's imagined world.

'We needed to develop the "future bleed" strand which leads to Sam betraying the team in the final episode. We talked right at the start of the writing process about ways of doing this. All sorts of ideas were chucked about. I even remember at one point suggesting that Sam should hallucinate a pig being butchered at odd moments during the show – a metaphor for the death of Gene! Dear God, what was I thinking? It would have been *Life On Mars* meets Peter Greenaway! I think we all felt much more confident about the tone

"At the last minute I suggested that the bus on which Sam and Gene find the murdered body should be destined for Hyde. No reason for it, really, but it got the conspiracy theorists frothing."

of the show in series two. We knew the weird stuff worked and people rather liked it. But you have to be careful not to overdo it. That's when it can become alienating or confusing, removing the audience from the story. Jane and Claire have always been very good at telling me when I've gone too far.'

Care to quote any examples?

'I once wrote a sequence where Sam imagined himself trapped in a Cyberman suit being pursued by Gene Hunt dressed as Jon Pertwee. Thank God I rationalized my senses and am feeling much better now. Having written quite a few LOMs I can say that you get a sense of when you've gone too far and what will work. I

knew in my bones that the Camberwick Green sequence was appropriate and Jane's reaction when I pitched it to her confirmed it. But the Cyberman, Gene Hunt driving Bessie in a tartan hacking jacket … you see what I'm saying?'

Yes, though must of us would now kill to see it.

Life On Mars was also packed full of tiny details and allusions. Taking Matthew's first episode as an example, Sam is being 'haunted' by the sound of gangster Tony Crane whistling 'Bring Me Sunshine' by his hospital bed in the future. Standing at the opening murder scene, the sound of Morecambe and Wise's signature tune echoing in his head, we notice the poster on the wall behind him.

'The Art Department found the original Eric and Ernie "Keep Britain Tidy" poster and it was of course a perfect match. Standing Sam and Gene in front of it just added that extra layer of cheekiness. Also at the last minute I suggested that the bus on which Sam and Gene find the murdered body should be destined for Hyde. No reason for it, really, but it got the conspiracy theorists frothing.'

Another tricky element to writing *Life On Mars* must be keeping the CID characters 'iconic'. The decision was made very early on that the show would never see Gene Hunt go home and live a life outside the office. Did that not make it a hard job keeping those characters fresh?

'If you look at the great TV drama series of the past you will tend to find that the characters don't change that much. Terry and George in *Minder*. Regan and Carter in *The Sweeney*. Audiences need to be familiar with the heroes and not have them change or evolve too much.

'Annie needed to come into CID because it was getting too hard finding ways of involving her in investigations. Obviously the Sam/Annie love story had to move forward. But Gene, Ray and Chris stay the same because they are ultimately

Above: Keep Britain Tidy or else!

constructs in Sam's mind – there is no reason for them to evolve because they serve a specific purpose: namely, they represent something for Sam to fight against. And besides, they're too much fun the way they are, I think!'

One thing that did change between series one and two was the decision to introduce important issues which had not really been touched on beforehand, such as racism.

'We always wanted to tackle seventies social issues but we were nervous of series one becoming "worthy". With series two we had a greater confidence, because we knew that if we explored a worthy issue we could always undermine it with some outrageous

*Left: Ray Emmet Brown as DC Glen Fletcher. **Middle:** Ravi (Paul Sharma) begs Toolbox (Ian Poulston-Davies) to tell him where he bought his shirt. **Right:** Patrick O'Brien (Brendan Mackey) awaits the inevitable kicking from Gene.*

CID business. It had also begun to feel like the elephant in the room, not tackling the IRA or the influx of Ugandan Asians. Writers like Guy Jenkin [episode six] really wanted to address that stuff and as long as they found a good story to frame it, we were happy. Guy's brilliant idea was to tie Ugandan Asians into Sam learning to let go of Maya, his Asian girlfriend in the present day.'

The fifth episode of the series saw another experiment in the writing formula. With Sam Tyler overdosing in his hospital bed the drama plays out partly in flashbacks and partly while he watches on a small monitor, having collapsed in the police station. This came about for purely practical reasons:

'John had worked tirelessly on series one, appearing – amazingly – in every single scene.

> **"There was even talk (one night after filming when oiled on cheap Bacardi substitute) that Gene could explode out of Sam's psyche and run amuck for real in our world. How bonkers is that?"**

That meant being on set by seven in the morning every day and not wrapping until seven at night. In addition he would then stumble off home and learn three or four scenes of dialogue for the next day. And Sam Tyler always had a lot to say for himself! John was wary of going through that again so I devised an episode that wouldn't require him all the time. He rarely got a full day off but sometimes a half day. I hope it made a bit of difference to him. By the time we came to episode five, all the cast were getting tired. It's that difficult stage of shooting where you still have as much to do again as you've already done. What was fun about it, necessity being the mother of invention and all that cobblers, was that in working out ways to extract Sam from the story I found a new way to *tell* the story, and I think I came up with some rather cool scenes as a result. I love it when Sam is watching the climax of the investigation on a portable TV whilst trapped inside the locker room because the doctors have dosed him with adrenalin-blockers and his mind has closed down.'

Matthew's joy in writing comes through as clearly on screen as it does when you meet him in person.

'I love to write. But then I've been writing scripts since I was twelve years old. Like those creepy little kids who learn the cello aged five and practise nine hours a day until they're in a symphony orchestra before they hit puberty, I just grew up with it. Writing is an extension of myself, it's as natural as eating. It is my most satisfying and consistent form of expression. People sometimes ask me what I would do if the writing work dried up. The answer is I would still write, but for myself. Of course you don't always feel like doing it. Rewrites can be tiresome. Tackling your eighth draft can be bloody infuriating. But little can compare to the feelings of expectation or anticipation when faced with sixty-five blank pages ready to be filled. A tip to disgruntled writers: always start the day with a scene that surprises – it gives your imagination a giddy-up. A good sex scene, perhaps. Or a car chase. Camberwick Green [the opening of the fifth episode where Sam imagines himself part of the children's animated series] was born out of the Monday morning blues.'

Halfway through filming the creative team had to decide whether to end Life On Mars after sixteen episodes or continue the narrative beyond. Everyone agreed that the most satisfying conclusion to the show would fall naturally at the end of series two.

'We had the ending worked out so it

SHOOTING SCRIPT EXTRACT - Episode 8

EXT. RAILWAY ARMS - DAY 8/3 - 1502
  SAM is met by ANNIE.
ANNIE: You okay?
SAM: Ask me; what should I do Annie?
ANNIE: Stay.
SAM: Yeah, all right then.
  He steps up, grabs her and snogs her face off with two series' worth of built-up passion. The moment is rudely broken by the Cortina crashing up onto the kerb. GENE jumps out.
GENE: Tyler, put that soppy plonk down 'n get in. Blag in Archer Lane. Shots fired. Lovely!
  RAY and CHRIS barrel out of the pub with fags in their gobs.
GENE: Get in you tarts! You too flash knickers!
  ANNIE goes in after RAY and CHRIS.
SAM: You're not driving with that leg Guv.
GENE: Yes I am.
SAM: You were shot!
GENE: So will you be if you don't get in.
  Everyone piles in the Cortina.
RADIO: No. It's no good. He's slipping away from us. Sam? Sam...?
SAM: Oh shut up. Hate that channel.
  SAM twists the dial until he gets David Bowie "Watch That Man".
SAM: That's better.
  GENE jumps behind the wheel.
SAM: I should be driving.
GENE: You drive like my Aunt Mabel.
SAM: If you injure someone in this car it's technically a criminal offence.
GENE: You noncey-arsed fairy boy!
SAM: Such graceful banter.
GENE: Pig off!
  He slams the car into first. The Cortina takes off away from us. SAM and GENE still arguing over Bowie.
SAM: Keep it under 70. And radio in for Uniform.
GENE: I don't need Plod in the way!
SAM: It's procedure! You're not above the law you know Guv!
GENE: What you on about Tyler? I AM the law!
SAM: In your dreams...
  The Cortina vanishes into a blaze of sunlight. Does it indeed actually vanish altogether?
  TEST CARD GIRL steps into view, smiling out at us from our TV sets. She reaches forward and switches off our tellys.
CUT TO BLACK.
THE END OF "LIFE ON MARS"

was just a question of making sure that all the storylines came together within the context of series two. The shoot-out in the tunnel was always going to be there but originally, when we planned for a possible series three, it would have ended on a cliffhanger with Sam disappearing into the blackness leaving the others to their fate. God, that would have driven people mad with righteous frustration.

Had that always been the intended conclusion?

'He was always in a coma and he was always going to wake up. But we were always discussing what might happen then to put another twist on it. One idea was that Gene followed him into 2007. Not the real Gene but a kind of imagined Gene. So that Sam is frustrated by red tape and imagines the Cortina smashing through it – riding to the rescue. There was even talk (one night after filming when oiled on cheap Bacardi substitute) that Gene could explode out of Sam's psyche and run amuck for real in our world. How bonkers is that? Actually it could have worked and been the springboard for a new series with Gene's Adventures in the Twenty-First Century. But it might have strayed too close to *New Tricks*.'

As it was, the show ended, as we all know, with Sam Tyler stepping off the roof of police headquarters, having realized that the world he struggled to return to for so long is not the one he wants to be in, and that the world of Gene and Annie, for all its faults, is the one he can't face losing. A brave decision, as it turned the lead character's suicide in effect into a moment of celebration.

> **"Sam's not really killing himself, he's sacrificing himself to save his friends. The way SJ Clarkson shot it, with the music and John's incredible determined smile, it just elevated a moment of defeat into a moment of victory."**

'I was never worried by it but our wonderful producer Cameron Roach did have concerns that we were being irresponsible. Of course *Life On Mars is* irresponsible in so many ways. This was just one more transgression. He's not really killing himself, he's *sacrificing* himself to save his friends. That's the healthiest way of looking at it. I think the BBC were a trifle nervous, even though they liked it. I guess it's the proper reaction, to be concerned. But the way SJ Clarkson shot it, with the music and John's incredible determined smile, it just elevated a moment of defeat into a moment of victory.'

That final episode was screened a week before transmission to a room full of journalists and luminaries at BAFTA; a chance for Matthew to gauge its success.

'I was enjoying the laughter in the room, so I knew the jokes were going down well. To be honest, I thought there were a lot of good vibes that night. I was so pleased with the episode but I was always braced for a mixed response. You're never going to please everyone. The science fiction fans in particular; I knew they'd want a more radical ending. But this was right for the character. This ending has emotional closure which would have been swamped by anything too outlandish or tricksy. I was amazed when they applauded the suicide and fade to black! They started cheering; they thought it was all over! At that moment I felt that if they were prepared to accept Sam's suicide then they'd probably love him coming to Gene's rescue in the tunnel.'

Despite the tangibly positive reaction to the show's conclusion there must have been a degree of sadness on Matthew's part to see it all over?

'I had mixed feelings. I almost cried, writing Sam waking up. I hated it. I didn't want him there. I like to write unnecessary stage directions in my scripts with pointlessly flowery descriptions – "If Sam Tyler were a flavour he would be spearmint", for example, from episode one of series one – but when I got back to 2007 my stage directions became spartan and matter-of-fact. Then again, it was hugely satisfying to return him to '73 and have that car drive off into the sunset. I secretly wanted the Cortina to take off like the end of *Grease*. Guess that would've been a bit camp.

'But you know what? Who says it's really all over?'

Certainly there is the follow-up, *Ashes To Ashes*, to look forward to, a show sprung from the brief scene at the end of *Life On Mars* where Sam records all of his experiences; experiences that could later be read and used to trigger a new 'visitor' to the world of Gene, Ray and Chris.

'Funnily enough, that scene was always going to be there. It was my mini homage to the end of *Alien*, when Ripley records her final thoughts and feelings before going into hyper-sleep. "This is Ripley, last survivor of the *Nostromo*, signing off." The words of the last survivor…

'Then we began to wonder whether Sam's psychologist could visit Gene and the gang. The idea began to catch fire. It was a chance to be doubly post-modern. Send someone who has effectively seen *Life On Mars* back in time to meet Gene Hunt.'

In the equally alien world of 1981. Time of string ties, neon pink, shiny suits, hairspray, frilly pirate shirts, neon pink, eyeliner, Flock of Bloody Seagulls and really really really bright neon pink… Gene won't know what hit him.

Right: The 'Future' of policing – DCI Gene Hunt in Ashes to Ashes

LOST AND FOUND:
A SLOW BUS TO NOWHERE

When they had woken up in the imaginary world of *Life On Mars* Adams and Thompson had filled their first few disorientating days by interviewing the officers of North West District CID. At every moment they had hoped that this shared illusion would vanish and they would find themselves back in the real world. Currently working as writer and photographer for the *Manchester Evening News* they were *still* hoping to be shot of this imagined 1973. The main reason Adams wished this right now was so that he might never see the smoke-bellowing Hillman Imp he had bought with their first paycheque ever again.

'Stupid bastard arse-wiping bugger turds!' he shouted, proving he was a literate wordsmith while trying to wrench the gear stick from second into third. It was refusing. It liked second. Second was a nice and steady gear.

'Everyone's going to have gone home by the time we get there,' Thompson moaned, rubbing the lens of his camera on his tank-top.

'This thing's got a mind of its own, we'll get there when it wants us to and not a moment before.' Adams sighed and resigned himself to tootling along at twenty-five: any more and the engine would likely vomit from the bonnet in a squeal of steam and metal.

They idled around a corner and saw the police tape and the sea of uniforms gathered about an empty double-decker bus. 'Here we go,' said Adams, and gracefully stalled the car as close to the kerb as he could. 'Gladys on the news desk says someone's had their head stoved in, so keep your camera ready – we want some money shots.'

'Yes, yes,' replied Thompson, irritably.

'Oh, look!' came a voice they both recognised. 'It's Pinky and Perky.'

'Morning, DC Carling,' Thompson said, ignoring the detective's mocking laugh.

'What can you tell us about this, then?' Adams said, pointing at the bus, his eyes drawn to the spider-web crack of an upstairs window, dark blood dulling the sun's reflection on the glass.

'Sod all. The Guv's made a statement: if you'd been here earlier you'd have 'eard it.'

'Yeah… Bet we didn't miss much though, eh? Come on, help us out here – you know we'll make you lot look better than most of the hacks.'

Carling frowned as he rumpled his moustache. He paused to light a cigarette. 'Middle-aged bloke, decent clobber, had his head smashed in with a hammer. Two blows here…' he tapped at his skull to indicate where the man had been hit. 'Plod's doing one of Tyler's stupid "swoops"…'

'He means "sweeps",' Thompson muttered, wandering away to take photographs.

'Whatever,' Carling huffed at Thompson's departing back. 'I'm off to talk to a couple of the usual suspects, see if anyone knows anything.'

'Thanks.' Adams finished scribbling in his notebook and shoved it in his jacket pocket. 'You're a star, owe you a pint.'

'Make it two.' Carling strolled towards his car and Adams hurried after Thompson in the direction of the stranded bus.

Thompson was rattling off shots of the blood-stained window as the sound of feet on the stairs inside made them both turn.

'Thanks, Annie,' said DI Tyler, watching the uniformed WPC jump from the bus and head back to the station.

'Sam.' Adams gave a half wave.

Tyler nodded, still looking at Annie. 'Alright, you two?'

'Yeah,' Thompson slipped his lens cap on and slung the camera back on his shoulder. 'Bloody marvellous.'

'Ask her out, you silly git,' Adams said, giving Tyler a wink.

It was the wrong thing to say. Tyler's face darkened. 'Mind your own business.' He walked off after Annie.

'Oops.' Adams rolled his eyes. 'Come on, let's go and get this written up.'

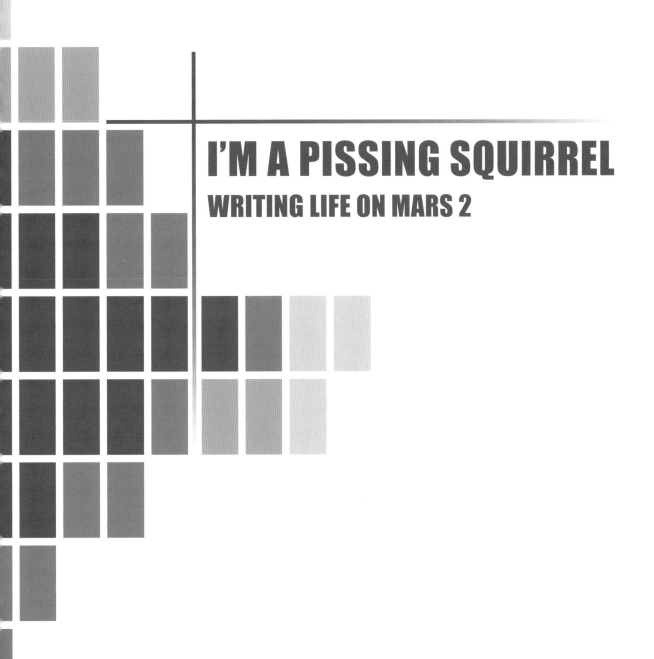

I'M A PISSING SQUIRREL
WRITING LIFE ON MARS 2

CHRIS CHIBNALL
WRITER, EPISODE 2

Chris Chibnall is a busy man. Much of his time is taken up with keeping an eye on that eclectic group of Cardiff-based investigators, *Torchwood*. Still, he found time to return to the world of *Life On Mars* to write the second episode of series two, which found Gene facing the unpleasant fact that his hero and mentor Superintendent Harry Woolf was a crook.

'Bent coppers – it's the most interesting aspect of seventies policing when you look back and read up on it. The really juicy character material always returns to the issue of corruption and coppers going bad: why they did it and where the line was drawn. I think that plays into the central notion of *Life On Mars*: how do you police what is right or wrong? It's the heart of the series.

'The great thing was to be able to see Sam's influence on Gene versus Harry's: how much they each play in the mix of his character, which one's going to triumph in the end; which one he feels most loyalty to. Gene says, "This is the way I was taught to do things," and that's very key to him, the way he still calls Harry "Guv" right up until the very end. That was the point of the story really, to challenge Gene and put him on the back foot.'

Over the course of the series there's no doubt that Gene changes some of his attitudes to policing.

'That's the great thing about the second series, watching Gene develop. It's almost imperceptible; then it

> **"That's the great thing about the second series, watching Gene develop. It's almost imperceptible; then it dawns on you that Sam is having an effect on him."**

dawns on you that Sam is having an effect on him. Of course Gene is also having an effect on Sam: the characters do shift gradually across those sixteen episodes.'

Unlike many shows on which writers are given a long 'shopping list' of plot threads and character development that they must consider when writing, Chris had a pretty free rein: 'There was very little in the way of a serial element to pick up on. The only thing was the phone call [to Sam, from his mysterious superior at 'Hyde' at the end of the episode] which we dropped in at the very end. The brief was very much to write a standalone episode which explored the two central characters. I think you have

SHOOTING SCRIPT EXTRACT - Episode 2

```
INT. CID - DAY 2/2
    GENE opens the door - and in walks
    DC GLEN FLETCHER. Late 20s, fresh
    faced, well turned out. Black.
    Cheery, eager to please. GLEN faces
    out RAY. Holds out a hand. RAY
    looks at it.
RAY: So you're here to do the
spadework
    Silence blankets the room. All eyes
    on GLEN. Doesn't flinch.
RAY: Only it can get quite cold round
here. It's not like being back at
home
GLEN: What, Burnage?
    A ripple of laughter. Ray is
    discomforted
SAM: You'll have to excuse DS Carling
- he's our resident Neanderthal.

GLEN: No, good point though. When
that heat wave hit last month, I
thought Enoch Powell had me deported!
    More laughter. Even RAY smiles.
GLEN: Still, don't worry - if there's
a power cut, I'll roll my eyes and
you can follow me to the exit
    More laughter. SAM looks on,
    horrified.
SAM: That's enough!
    His shout silences everyone.
SAM: You don't have to play Uncle
Tom to fit in here. You're better than
that.
GLEN: (Beat) Hold up. DI Tyler.
(Another beat) You were at Hyde.
```

to be very careful in the early episodes of any series to make sure you don't rock the boat too much, to make sure you stick to stating the core values of the show. The later episodes can play about a bit more; they can be a little odd and edgier. This was just a police romp!'

A change in schedule did result in an unplanned link between the first two episodes, however: 'It was originally planned to be the third transmitted episode but then got moved to the second. Once we'd realised it would be filming in the same block as episode one and that actor Kevin McNally would be available, Matthew changed a scene featuring a random police commissioner so that Woolf appeared [in the first episode as well as the second], making the audience think he would be a regular. Pure red herring stuff – God bless Matthew for that.'

Despite his workload it's obvious that Chris enjoyed his return to seventies Manchester.

'Some shows are harder to write than others. I found *Life On Mars* to be the most enjoyable show I'd ever written for. You go a long way just with the characters of Sam and Gene. Beneath its clever and elegant set-up the series is surprisingly simple: it's a buddy cop movie, and that's always a joy to write.'

JULIE RUTTERFORD
WRITER, EPISODE 3

Julie Rutterford is a writer of variety. From twenties period sleuth *Mrs Bradley* to the feckless skivers of *Shameless* her CV is nothing if not broad. Her story of Irish immigrants, car bombs (red wire … yellow wire?) and Post Traumatic Stress Disorder is business as usual, then. How did she get commissioned for the show?

'I slept with … no, wrong series. I'd worked for Kudos before on the second series of *Hustle*, so it was nice to be approached again by them.'

Julie is the only woman to ever write an episode of *Life On Mars*, a show that, metaphorically speaking, fairly reeks of male body odour. Did she feel the need to shower afterwards?

'Strangely enough I found it easier to write for Gene Hunt than quite a few female characters I'd written for previously, but I think that's because he was so wonderfully drawn by his creators, Matthew, Ashley and Tony. I admire his ability to punch his way through endless red tape whilst keeping a ciggie on the go.'

Several of the other writers have talked about juggling the right amount of realism with a lighter touch. Does Julie think that a format like *Life On Mars* – most particularly owing to its elements of fantasy and humour – is a good one for dealing with something a little more weighty?

'Yes, I personally think it is an ideal vehicle for such issues. Issue-led dramas are sometimes weighed down by their own gravitas – a point can be made more succinctly through fantasy and, especially, humour.

'The story was originally about the bombing campaign by the IRA on mainland Britain in 1973 – what if someone were to use that as a smokescreen for another crime? The issue of the treatment of Irish immigrants evolved naturally from that – the smokescreen only became possible because at the time of the bombings (and, in fact,

> **"Strangely enough I found it easier to write for Gene Hunt than quite a few female characters I'd written for previously, but I think that's because he was so wonderfully drawn by his creators."**

long before that) there was a lot of anti-Irish feeling in Britain, especially in areas with large Irish communities, such as Manchester, where at one time it was common to see signs up that read, "No Blacks, No Irish."'

Despite its darker side there is still a great deal of nostalgia for the period of the show. Could she see herself living in 1973?

'Yes,' she replies, without a moment's hesitation. 'Liverpool used to win the League back then!'

Frank Miller, the building site foreman and attempted bank robber from Julie's script, shares his name with the renowned comics writer and artist who heralded a new era with *Batman: The Dark Knight Returns* in the eighties and who was responsible, amongst many other works, for the original books from which the movies *Sin City* and *300* were adapted. Comics fan or coincidence?

'Both! I wrote an original drama a few years ago where the main character was a graphic novelist and artist. I knew about *Ghost World* by Daniel Clowes but once I'd started the research, I became a big fan – especially of *Ice Haven* and *Art School Confidential*. So I have read a bit about Frank Miller but my personal favourite remains Daniel Clowes – I even own an Enid Coleslaw doll [the heroine of *Ghost World* as played by Thora Birch in the movie adaptation].

One final question. Red wire, yellow wire?

'Red.'

Ashley Pharoah
Writer, Episode 4 + Co-Creator

The fourth episode of the second series sees the return of co-creator Ashley Pharoah to the world of *Life On Mars*. Was he energized by the success of the first series or intimidated?

'Without a doubt, energized! It was easier to write the second series, knowing the actors' voices and mannerisms, their strengths. And to do that with the security of knowing that people loved our little show was very exciting.'

Both Ashley and his fellow writer and co-creator (along with Tony Jordan) Matthew Graham have been frank in their surprise at the show's success. 'I suppose so many people in rather good Armani suits had told us for the last eight years that it was a silly idea and wouldn't work on mainstream television. Also, we British are obsessed by social realism, we tend to think that if drama isn't about postmen, striking miners or doctors it isn't real. This was a high-concept show that couldn't survive on decent reviews alone; it had to get millions of people engaged. So we were nervous and I think we were right to be nervous! Looking back, of course, it seems like a no-brainer.'

How vital was the element of humour to that success?

'It's not so much that the humour is important to the show as the juxtaposition of that humour with tragedy, emotion, weirdness. I think that's the strength of *Life On Mars*, that variety in tone within the same episode – sometimes within the same scene. Writing it was a challenge but also a joy, a lovely release from the straightjackets of both realism and genre.'

Although it may have escaped gleefully from those twin straightjackets *Life On Mars* nonetheless has its feet firmly set in realism of a sort, its stories grounded in problems that were very much part of everyday life in 1973. Football hooliganism, the death of heavy industry and the treatment of women were all themes that figured in first season episodes; while season two tackled other issues that made headlines in the seventies – racism, heroin and the IRA.

'It was always a fine balance between the *reality* of 1973 and the *ironic* look at 1973 through a contemporary sensibility – which is what we were actually doing. *Life On Mars* isn't, after all, a documentary. It's our – and Sam's – interpretation of 1973.'

Ashley's work can often be defined by his exemplary handling of female characters.

'I love writing for female characters. In that particular episode

> **"I love writing female characters. In that particular episode I really wanted Sam to feel the absence of women who loved him. No mother at his bedside. No voices seeping through TVs, etcetera. Real loneliness."**

INT. TWILLING HOUSE. NIGHT 4/6 - 2015
*Carol starts to take her clothes off,
neatly handing them to one of the Toga
Girls.*
*Sam and Annie (under the aliases of
Tony and Cherie Blair) freeze.*
Oh my God.
*Then Mrs Luckhurst and Barbara start
to unbutton their clothes.*
ROGER: (To Annie) Don't be shy, Cherie.
*Annie manages a smile. Takes a deep
breath. And starts to unbutton her
shirt. Sam doesn't know where to look,
is very uncomfortable.*
*Suddenly there is the noise of the
front door opening and then Gene
strides into the room. He is holding
the hands of a pretty, tarty woman
called SUKI.*
GENE: I see you've started without me.
ROGER: Who the hell are you?
GENE: (To Sam) You didn't tell them we
were coming?
Everyone looks at Sam.
SAM: (Thinking quickly) I thought you'd
chickened out. This is my friend,
Gordon... Brown. And his wife...
SUKI: Suki.
*Suki starts to take her clothes off
without being told.*
Roger is very suspicious.
ROGER: Whoa there. This is an invite-
only party.
GENE: (Indicates Sam) He invited me.
SAM: I'm sorry, Roger. Gordon's a good
friend, I was excited, I let it slip.
GENE: I like a party. I'm very discreet.
ROGER: (Steely, to Sam) This is my house,
Tony. I say who gets invited here.
SAM: I'm sorry, you're right. I think
we should go.
ANNIE: No.
They all look at Annie.
ANNIE: If you go you go without me. I'm
enjoying myself.
Mrs Luckhurst looks Gene up and down.
MRS LUCKHURST: I think Mr Brown should
be allowed to stay.
GENE: Thank you. Mrs...?
MRS LUCKHURST: Mrs Luckhurst.
Gene swallows.

Above: *Roger Twilling (Nicholas Palliser) admires an opportunity.*

I really wanted Sam to feel the absence of women who loved him. No mother at his bedside. No voices seeping through TVs, etcetera. Real loneliness. Just Gene and Chris and Ray and pubs. I like it that he says, "I'm bloody sick of 1973." So I had the idea that a beloved aunt was visiting him in hospital in the present, and it was the smell of her perfume that inspired his imagination into thinking up the wife-swapping story. Sam is truly sick of the way women are treated in 1973. And Annie grows, too; steps up to the plate as a strong woman.'

On the subject of perfume, those 'Beauvoir Ladies' seem awfully familiar...?

'They were always meant to be Avon Ladies. I have such searing memories of them coming to my house and trying to flog my mum cosmetics she didn't want or couldn't afford but was too polite to say so. A heady mix of perfume and smiling, made-up women. Avon were happy for us to use the name but I think some BBC lawyers got a bit nervous.'

Making television programmes will always be affected by red tape of course; it is simply the way things must be done. Policing is no different and many viewers seem to hanker nostalgically for the age of Gene Hunt and his blunt-nosed attitude to such things. Is there an argument for that style of policing? Were things really better back then?

'I suppose it was a tad simpler as coppers tended to know the villains personally. It was a matter of finding enough evidence to send them down, rather than the faceless crimes of today. But there were too many miscarriages of justices, too many mistakes. The biggest one was letting themselves be seen as the private army of the party in power. People who get misty-eyed about that style of policing should remember the role of the Met during the miners' strike. I think it's funny to watch in *Life On Mars* but only in a thank-God-its-not-1973 way.'

Still, surely he and Gene Hunt would get on?

'We'd be okay as long as we talked about beer – like most men. Nah … he'd hate me: pouffy Southern bastard who prefers rugby to football; actually quite likes being with women; eats the occasional vegetable; reads novels; has at least made a game attempt at finding the G-spot. Oh, and can't drive. He would *loathe* me.'

Was it sad to finish the show?

'Very sad, actually. Personally, I would have *loved* to have done a Christmas two-parter, with lots of Mud and Morecambe and Wise, Chocolate Oranges and Scotsmac.'

Ashley is clearly a man with a penchant for the era, his episode standing as possibly the most Blue Nun-drenched slice of seventies recreation the series ever saw. What would be his preferred vol-au-vent filling?

'Er… Can you get cider to stay inside a vol-au-vent?'

It would be certainly worth the effort. Perhaps, if he ate enough of them, he might be tempted to try a little partner-swapping himself with the cast and crew. Who would he get stitched up with in that event?

'Matthew.'

On which note, I think we'd best leave them in peace.

> **"I would have *loved* to have done a Christmas two-parter, with lots of Mud and Morecambe and Wise, Chocolate Oranges and Scotsmac."**

GUY JENKIN
WRITER, EPISODE 6

Guy Jenkin has an illustrious string of credits to his name. A stalwart of political comedy, from *Drop the Dead Donkey*, *Spitting Image* and *Not the Nine O'Clock News* through to modern pieces such as *Sex 'n' Death* and *Jeffery Archer: The Truth* (which had the wonderful tagline: 'This story is based on real events. Only the facts have been changed.') both of which he also directed. How then did he come to enter the world of seventies Manchester?

'I knew Jane Featherstone at Kudos because she had produced a couple of projects of mine. I'd told her I was a big fan of the first series, so she asked me if I was interested in writing an episode.'

Was writing the show as much fun as he had expected?

'I don't ever expect a writing job is going to be fun. But I was keen to write for those two actors and those two characters. They're both terrific in different ways. With John Simm you can see every emotion on his face. He's almost see-through as an actor – in a brilliant way. Phil Glenister can take the most 'written' line, keep it very funny, but make it not seem written any more.'

'As nervous as a very small nun at a Penguin shoot,' for example?

'That was one of my favourites. It's a very *written* line but he makes it not sound as though it is. He makes it sound natural. He'd been in an episode of *Drop the Dead Donkey* about fifteen years before, playing a psychotic policeman,

Above: Toolbox Terry says 'Name That Tune in three'.

so he was very much in the same role. The character's so good, too; as a seventies cop he can say things that wouldn't be considered acceptable today.

'British TV rarely does things that are larger than life and have such a big premise as *Life On Mars*. When I first heard about it I presumed it was a comedy because it *sounds* like a comedy. It took me fifteen minutes to figure out what was going on when I watched the first episode. They were playing it dead straight. It is funny but it's played absolutely truthfully. As a style of writing, I really like that.'

Guy's episode is also notable for reintroducing – and effectively writing out – Sam's girlfriend in the present, Maya. Was that something that came with the brief?

'No, that was my idea. When I decided to write something involving Ugandan Asian immigrants, it worked naturally with that. One of the things that made the show so attractive for writers is that Kudos are good at giving the writer a great deal of independence. You have to follow the general plot of the series, of course, but the stories can also exist pretty much on their own. The Maya storyline did, however, fit neatly with the need to move Sam on from that relationship so that he could develop his feelings for Annie.'

The episode also features armed robber turned drug smuggler, Toolbox Terry, and his intimidating partner, Big Bird. 'They were quite unusual, I suppose. But then there were some quite unusual characters in it to start with!'

Having directed so much of his own work in recent years, did he find it difficult giving up that level of control for *Life On Mars*?

'It's fine as long as you don't get *at all* involved. If you get a *bit* involved, you'll want to get involved a lot more. If it's something you've invented yourself, you'll want to see it all the way through, put your vision on the screen; but this is someone else's world, so it wasn't that hard.'

MARK GREIG
WRITER, EPISODE 7

Gene on the run, dressed as Tufty the Road Safety Squirrel. Bound to happen sooner or later, wasn't it? For those finding their childhood memories particularly bruised by this vision, it's all Mark Greig's fault: 'I was a kid in the seventies, and the first thing I thought of about that era was Tufty. Which may say more about my feelings for furry creatures than it may be wise to make public. A road safety superhero…'

How did Mark come to introduce Tufty to *Life On Mars*? 'I had the extraordinarily good fortune to work with Claire Parker as my first ever script editor on my first ever TV gig, which was an episode of *Taggart*. We'd kept in touch, and when an episode unexpectedly came available on the first series of *Life On Mars*, she asked if I'd like to do it. I turned it down, having already committed to the excellent *Afterlife*. After having seen the first series become not just a hit but a part of television history, I felt like the fool I have always secretly suspected I am. I was very happy – indeed, pathetically grateful – when she refused to take rejection as a gross personal insult and asked if I'd like to do an episode for the second series.'

There's an impressive list of crime on Mark's CV. *The Bill*, *Taggart*, *Rebus*, *Inspector Lynley*… But while *Life On Mars* may look like a crime show on the surface, it was decided early on in the first series that the crime plots themselves should be kept simple, since there was so much else in the mix that otherwise the stories threatened to become unwieldy. Was that the case with Mark?

'I have done a lot of crime,' he agrees. 'Writers get typecast as much as actors and my type seems to have been set as "he does dark"; but I am interested in the moral choices characters make, and criminals do make interesting moral choices. I would say *Life On Mars* was part of the crime genre – its own absurdist metaphysical sub-

SHOOTING SCRIPT EXTRACT - Episode 7

INT. SAM'S FLAT. BEDROOM - DAY 7/4
   *Sam, having been sleeping on the
   floor, SCREAMS and bolts upright.
   Gene's apprehended half-way through
   a snore - chokes, tumbles out of
   Sam's bed.
   He wears only pants.*
GENE: Jesus! What, what, who, what?
   *Sam realizes it was just a dream,
   but one he doesn't want to share
   the details of.*
SAM: Nothing. Sorry. A dream.
GENE: What I call a dream involves
Diana Dors and a bottle of chip oil.
Oh no. That was a guilty conscience
my friend.
SAM: What?
GENE: The root of nightmares.
SAM: My conscience is clear.
GENE: Whereas me - slept like a baby.
   Sam pulls on his trousers.
SAM: A twenty stone baby that sweats,
farts and snores.
GENE: I do not snore.

Below: Director SJ Clarkson finds one of the production team dead on set.

33

genre perhaps, but definitely part of the crime story family. The "inbred cousin kept locked in the cellar who may or may not have telepathic powers" part of the crime family, maybe. The crime stories were necessarily simple because of the sheer amount of colourful character and contextual stuff they had to carry, but I felt that they provided the solid structure that kept the narrative moving through the weirder bits.'

All of the show's writers have commented on the amount of creative autonomy that Kudos was willing to give them. Not only did Mark have one of the main characters on the run as a murder suspect but he also introduced Detective Inspector Frank Morgan, who would become integral to the climax of the show. How much did he have to work to a given brief?

'I've been lucky in that most of my writing experiences have involved quite a lot of freedom, largely due to the fact that I've done several self-contained longer-form dramas, or worked with companies with whom I have a good relationship, which I think means they trust me not to screw it up. As far as I can remember – which isn't far at all, usually – the brief from Kudos was that episode seven should take Sam to a pretty dark place. My initial pitch – Gene on the run and suspected of murder – featured the reappearance of Sam's father and a *very* dark place indeed, but over a couple of story conferences we decided that wouldn't work: it was a step too far. We felt that Sam needed to either *go* to Hyde or be *visited* by someone from Hyde. We plumped for the latter, and that visitor

became Frank Morgan.

'After that I was off, and in good shape until late in the day, when the greyhound-betting milieu the story was originally set in was scuppered because a convincingly period greyhound track couldn't be found near enough to the production base. So the background was hastily changed to boxing – with me screaming about how much last-minute rewriting it would involve – and the episode was vastly improved for it. Which shows how much I know.'

Guy Jenkin said that he never expected writing to be fun but that he enjoyed writing for *Life On Mars* 'as much as one *could* ever enjoy a writing job.' Does writing give Mark pleasure? Can it ever actually be 'fun'?

'Good bloody question. The short answer has to be, by any objective measure, no. The long answer is: unless your idea of fun is working under enormous pressure in conditions more or less guaranteed to increase feelings of insecurity and inadequacy, and in the certain knowledge that the bits you like best will inevitably be cut – I think because those bits are kind of self-indulgent curlicues that aren't *really* part of the relentless necessity to JUST TELL THE BLOODY STORY – then no, it's not fun. There are moments when you get totally absorbed into your fictional universe and it all seems to flow; or when you have a surprising and unexpected insight into a character or story, or when you come up with a moment that you just *know* is going to take the audience by surprise and you get a gleeful rush; but on the whole it's a hard slog. A hard bloody slog I am driven to do. Playing in sand dunes is

> "I was a kid in the seventies, and the first thing I thought of about that era was Tufty. Which may say more about my feelings for furry creatures than it may be wise to make public. A road safety superhero..."

Above: Gene does his bit for road safety, with help from the costume team and director SJ Clarkson (top right).

fun; writing is not. Having said that, *Life On Mars* was a blast and a blessed release after years of conventional cop shows. Best of all, I got to be funny, which was both liberation and revelation for me. Which isn't to say my favourite lines didn't get cut, because of course they did; they always do. I still mourn the loss of "I'm a pissing squirrel". Kept me amused for weeks, that line. It's a lonely life, writing…'

Unsurprisingly, that lost line was one of Gene's. How difficult a character is he to write for? Is it a challenge to keep him as vulgar and expressive as viewers would expect (including his never-ending supply of similes) without being repetitive?

'I cursed the bastard constantly, particularly his sodding similes. My comic taste tends to the visual and the absurd, so my angle was to stress that and place the similes artfully.'

His conversational style aside, what is Mark's take on Hunt's style of policing?

'I can see how it might seem attractive, and from what I've heard he's a paragon of virtue compared to some coppers from that era; but I think his attractiveness stems from our own nostalgia for a time when things seemed simpler. Policing reflects the crime it combats, and if he tried the same methods now it wouldn't be long before he ended up in court or with a bullet in his head. Put him up against today's ruthless and sophisticated criminals and he'd look a complete twat. I don't like him much. I wouldn't want to spend an evening in the pub with him. I am a mimsy pinko after all.'

LOST AND FOUND:
THE ONE THAT GOT AWAY

'Bloody hell!'

It was a week later and Adams and Thompson had been trying to cheer themselves up with an Indian. Hot, spicy and possibly filled with household pets, it was the closest they got to a treat on their wages. Seeing someone thrown from a car outside the restaurant came by way of dessert.

Running towards the groaning man Thompson found himself reaching into a jacket pocket for a mobile phone that was no longer there – something he did frequently. He dropped to his haunches by the body, a moustachioed black guy with bruises that were going to feel twice as sore by tomorrow.

'Are you alright?' he asked, not really knowing what else to say.

The black guy drew in a pained breath and put his hand to his head. 'Need to call the station.'

Thompson nearly said 'Why? You got a train to catch?' but managed to stop himself. He looked up to see Adams still staring down the road after the fleeing vehicle.

'You know who was in that car?' he said. 'Superintendent Woolf.'

'Oh…' Thompson wasn't sure how he felt about that. He reached into the injured man's jacket and pulled out his wallet and warrant card. 'Detective Constable Glenn Fletcher,' he announced.

'Policing's always been a bit frisky round here but I don't remember them throwing each other out of cars before,' Adams said. 'I'd better call the station. Keep an eye on him.'

'Wait,' Fletcher croaked. 'I'll do it.' He pressed his fist against his temple and growled.

'Get back on your feet first, pal. We're mates with CID, y'know.' Adams was eager to get involved.

'Just tell 'em the one I was with got away, then, don't name any names.'

Adams shrugged. This wasn't the time to argue. 'Okay.'

He ran back across to the restaurant, and made a grab for their phone. 'Emergency, need to call the police,' he said to the startled waiter. He pressed his hand tight to his free ear, trying to drown out the noise of sitar music. He heard a familiar voice answer. 'Phyllis!' he shouted. 'One of your lot's just been thrown from a car: DS Glen Fletcher…' He held the phone away from his ear for a moment as the Desk Sergeant shouted back.

Outside Thompson was helping Fletcher to his feet. 'Take it easy, you might have concussion,' he said.
'And the rest. I need to get back to the station… Have you got a car?'
Thompson bit his lip awkwardly. 'Sort of…'

The Hillman Imp tore along the road like a Sloth with a broken leg, DS Fletcher getting ever more impatient in the back seat. 'Can't you go any faster?'
'Not really,' Adams answered, testing the accelerator pedal and causing a wad of black smoke to be spat from the exhaust like phlegm.

They sighed to a halt outside the station and Fletcher was out and on the run before Adams had even got the handbrake on. 'Come on then!' Adams shouted to Thompson, clambering out.
'Why?' replied Thompson. 'It's nothing to do with us any more … you're acting like we're a part of all that.' He gestured at the concrete beehive that housed the division. 'It's not as if we'd even get past the desk.'
Adams sank back to the driving seat, legs hanging out of the door. 'I just want to be doing … *something*.'
Thompson sighed. 'I know. Let's go home.'
Adams looked at him but didn't say anything. He put the car in gear and they drove away.

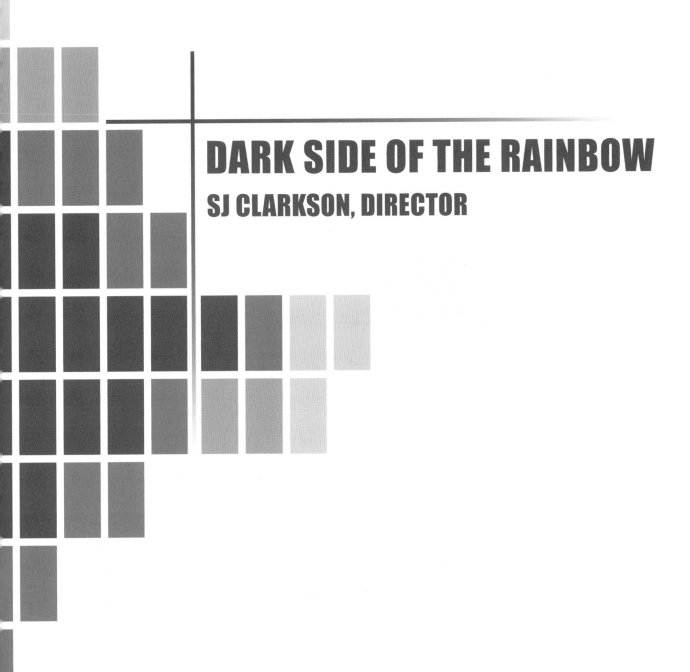

DARK SIDE OF THE RAINBOW
SJ CLARKSON, DIRECTOR

In series one, SJ Clarkson gave us rival football gangs with Gene Hunt as an undercover pub landlord in the fifth episode, and a death in custody in the seventh. When it came to selecting directors for the second series she was invited to direct four episodes, opening and closing the series with her own dynamic touch. Combining an instinctual head for technical detail with a determination to keep the emotional troubles of Sam Tyler to the fore, she welcomed us back to seventies Manchester and then powerfully closed the door on the world of *Life On Mars* as we know it forever.

Directing is a dream occupation for SJ and something she seems to have been building towards from a very young age.

'I've always been absolutely fascinated by films, *The Wizard of Oz* being one of my earliest memories of movies. As a child I remember my parents taking me to see *Tarka the Otter* and I ended up sobbing, wondering how something could make me feel like that. It wasn't just film: I was into the theatre, music; all the arts really. I started off in theatre, though, working for Cameron Mackintosh, who produced *Phantom of the Opera*, *Les Misérables*, *Miss Saigon*, all those big musicals. I was his office junior for a year before starting a career in stage management. It was while I was working in stage management on productions in the West End that I began to think about film again. Because I worked in the evening I went to the cinema in the day. I think there was a period where I saw every film going.

'I was also into animation and I thought for a while I might try and become an animator. I did a course in animation in New York and soon realised it wasn't for me. It took me all morning to draw twelve images of a ball bouncing and then all afternoon to shoot them. They went to the labs to be developed overnight and then when I came back in the morning and watched the rushes it lasted one second. I can't wait that long for so little – a *day's work* for a second! My hat goes off to animators because I think they are an extraordinarily talented bunch of people; but it can also be a very lonely job. I'm sure you can work with big teams of animators; but we spent so much time doing pencil and line drawings where it's just you and the paper. It did teach me the value of story boarding though, and I still really enjoy story boarding many of the scenes that I work on.

'One day, we went to Central Park and did stop motion animation using this guy jumping off a wall. It took all day but then we had fifty seconds of this guy literally flying through the air. That was so much more fun, working in a team and seeing something you wouldn't see in a normal life – that was magical. I realised that was closer to what I wanted to do.

'To earn some money and pay off my debt from film school I got a job temping in the factual department at the BBC. They really encouraged my ambitions and I ended up doing some filming for The Holiday Programme, and from there I moved over to drama.'

Following this SJ worked on a number of popular returning dramas, gaining a reputation as someone who enjoyed working with actors and delivered episodes with a strong visual flair.

'My agent knew I wanted to work for Kudos because I was a big fan of *Spooks* and *Hustle*. He told me that there was a new show coming up called *Life On Mars*. They sent me a script, I read it and I was desperate to do it. I haven't read another script to date where I have so engaged with it, where I could literally *see* it, respond to it and connect with it. That doesn't happen often. You get a script and you think, "Okay, how am I going to tackle this?" This just jumped out at me.

And having thrived working on series

> **"I was delighted to be returning: I loved the show and the characters; I got on well with the artists. Also, I hadn't directed one of Matthew's scripts, which I'd really wanted to do."**

one, SJ was keen to build on the series further by becoming the lead director, and a core member of the team on series two.

'Obviously I was delighted to be returning: I loved the show and the characters; I got on well with the artists. Also, I hadn't directed one of Matthew's scripts, which I'd really wanted to do; in the first series I'd directed an episode by Tony Jordan and one by Chris Chibnall – whom I adore – and Chris had written episode two, so that was exciting, too.

'It was a challenge, though, because we hadn't even transmitted the first episode of series one at that point. As the show began to transmit it was getting an amazing reception; we soon realised that the show was big, it wasn't just a little cult show that we loved: people were talking about it. All these things go through your head: *they've asked me to come back and*

*Opposite: John Simm, SJ Clarkson and Phil Glenister on the CID set during episode seven. **Above:** With John Simm and Phil Glenister on the lost and found set, also from episode seven.*

Above top: Liz White and John Simm share a chuckle on set with Phil Glenister before shooting their big kiss.
Above middle: All strapped up – the Cortina prepped for a close-up shot of the inside of the car for the final sequence
Above bottom: Designer Matt Gant clings to the Test Card Girl's clown whilst the massive crane is set up behind him.

Opposite Page: The crane used to achieve the final iconic shot of the series is set up ready for filming.

open this hit show … I hope I don't screw it up!

'Still, I knew what worked from series one and what didn't. I felt that episode seven of that first series was a nod to where the show should go, it felt a bit darker. The thing that works for *Life On Mars* in my opinion is the *truth* of it and that's a testament to John Simm. Imagine how stupid you would feel screaming at your TV, even in the privacy of your own home. To do that in front of a crew of thirty-five people – and do it so brilliantly – is amazing. I am absolutely in awe of John, he's terrific, to keep pulling that off and find the truth in every scene.

'I was determined that it was this element – the truth – that we should keep striving for. As much as this is a great high concept show, as much as there are car chases and action, what would you do if you woke up in 1973? As soon as you think about that properly it stops being a joke. You really would think you were going mad. Just imagine if you genuinely found yourself in a different *time*! I was constantly saying to John to keep that in mind. John and I knew that Sam must never get comfortable; the minute he gets comfortable the audience would stop caring. You must always feel the jeopardy: this isn't just another laugh. He needs to get out. Why is he there? What's going on in this man's head? The minute he accepts it all, where's the drama? Then you're just making *The Sweeney*.'

So how does a director approach the job?

'You get involved as early as you can. On a TV drama you have between five and eight weeks preparation, in which you get to know the show. On the first series I talked to Bharat and really worked at understanding the grammar of the show. Preparation always seems to be three and half weeks getting a feel for it, watching relevant films and so forth, then one and a half weeks of madness because often the scripts are still being worked on. Still, I think a script *should* be a fluid thing, constantly changing, constantly moving. The entire editorial team would continually question the script, right up until the day of the shoot.

'The same goes during filming: things come up,

opportunities occur – and it's about learning when and how to embrace them. There's no strict formula for making a scene work, it depends on so many circumstances: performances, the vibe at the time, and sometimes even the weather – for example the sequence in the final episode where Sam meets Morgan at the graveyard, we were shooting on a day where it was raining one moment and bright sunshine the next; Tim Palmer (the director of photography) and I decided we should go with the rain because it added so much to the sequence, but it did mean that the incredible art department were having to spray water over the car throughout the Sam-Morgan interior car dialogue. You can see how much the rain adds to the sequence in the final cut though!

'The great thing about series two was that I was brought in really early – on the second draft of the scripts – and there were storyline meetings which I was invited to. That makes the director feel very central in the creative process – a real collaborator on the show. You get under the skin of the script, start to feel how you can bring it to life and create the atmosphere it offers.'

How much does a director rely on his or her vision of what the writer wants to say? Is it something that requires constant referral to the writer, or something she just runs with?

'It's instinct. You hope you *instinctively* know what the scene is trying to say. If you don't, then you question it over and over until you can make it work in your head. Often writers are so imaginative that they write wonderful ideas which read terrifically well but which in real terms are impossible to film. I think a director's job is to come in and take on board the essence of the script, and then bring it to life. There is the clichéd example of the stage direction, "the *Titanic* sinks". That's not what you want to see, just a boat disappearing underwater. You want to see tables turning, people scrabbling, a hand grabbing onto a railing, books flying off shelves,

water seeping through holes in the hull … it's all *those* things that the scene needs to bring it to life on the screen.

'To use episode eight as an example: Matthew really didn't want the present to be appealing, he wanted it to be just empty and cold; drab and dreary, a place Sam no longer felt comfortable – if he ever did. So the script details directions like: *Sam walks down a busy shopping street, Sam sits by the side of the road* … things like that. My job is then finding a way of conveying the atmosphere Matthew's after, finding the locations that will tell that part of the story. The sequence needed to be long enough to get a sense of what was wrong: why it wasn't working for him, how much of a misfit he was now in the future; to show that he had actually learned from 1973 and saw things now through different eyes. Still, we didn't want to

stay *too* long in the future because you don't want people disappointed, thinking it was a real downbeat ending. Again, it comes down to instinct. As soon as I had the look and the feel of 2007, that was enough, and it was time to move on.

'Another thing that we wanted to achieve was that from the minute Sam wakes up, you needed the audience to feel that every scene was going to be the last. That was hard, as you had to try and give each scene a climax, while still taking the audience on a continual journey and not making it feel as if it kept stopping and starting. Also, I felt not only duty bound but a sheer *necessity* to mirror what Bharat had done in the opening of the first series. We had to bookend it. I timed the tracking shot Bharat

"From the minute Sam wakes up, you needed the audience to feel that every scene was going to be the last. That was hard, as you had to try and give each scene a climax, while still taking the audience on a continual journey."

used around Sam when he first woke up in 1973 – thirty-seven seconds – and shot mine for the same length, but moving the camera in the opposite direction. Bharat started with a tight shot on Sam's face and then zoomed out; I started wide and zoomed in. I wanted to give it a full circle, make it feel like one big story with the coda at the end where he goes back to 1973.

'It was the same on the first episode of the second series. I really wanted it to be episode nine if you like, a direct continuation from that first run of eight episodes. To make the series work I felt it had to be a direct follow-up, otherwise you would want to know what Sam's been doing while the series was off air; and as we experience *everything* through him I didn't want that. We couldn't get the bed back from the hire company that was used in series one, so Matt [Gant, the designer] had to build an exact replica, because I insisted that nothing could change. Those little attentions to detail were what I thought would make it.'

In fact some of SJ's details are astounding, even down to dropping 'flash frames' (really brief shots) into her episodes that foreshadow events to come.

'In the first episode I wanted to tease the audience a little, maybe make them think Sam was waking up; so there were flash frames of the hospital room, almost subliminal. I made sure the room had the same blinds as CID, that same square-patterned ceiling. It was the same set as Sam's bedroom in 1973, so it had the same shape but with elements of the office thrown in.

You hardly see it. But that detail needs to be there.

'In the final episode, when Sam has been talking to Annie, I dropped in flash frames of the railway track, too – if he's making all this up then there's no reason why he shouldn't know what's going to happen – to show how fragmented his state of mind was.'

The use of colour was also very important to SJ, working carefully with colourist Jet Omoshebi to create a palette that gave the episodes the atmosphere she was after.

'Whether anyone notices, other than me or the production team, doesn't even matter. It gives it uniformity. If you allow yourself to go on creative tangents too much it can become a mess. That makes it sound like we're

> **"I had a strong belief in using colours to describe an episode. The early episodes were warmer; later we used green a lot more: we chose a specific film stock to make it greener."**

limited, but it's not that at all; you have to be *intensely* creative but at the same time rein yourself in, otherwise you could have ended up with anything and everything in this show.

'I had a strong belief in using colours to describe an episode. The early episodes were a little warmer than the later ones, a bit of red – not too much, I'm not a fan of red on screen – but red is associated with danger, so Tony Crane and the Casino had that feel. Other than that I think the Test Card Girl is the only red you should see. In the later episodes we used green a lot more: we chose a specific film stock to make it greener. When Morgan [the DCI who, in Sam's fantasy, has sent him undercover to destroy Gene Hunt] came in and ran CID more tidily than Gene had done, we shot everything in a linear and symmetrical way, something we weren't used to on *Life On Mars*. We changed the lighting too. Episode seven was like a pre-op, with eight as

This page: Filming happens – come rain (above in a sequence from episode seven) or shine (right, from the dramatic 'leap of faith' in episode eight).

Opposite Page: Hitting slate 600 on set during episode seven, SJ Clarkson with director of photography Tim Palmer.

real. I must admit I started doubting it myself! Matthew Graham's so clever; I read it about ten times to get it straight. A great scene, because it made me question and analyze.'

Similarly SJ agonized about the final sequence of the series – in the end she achieved the impressive final shot of the Cortina driving off; a complex shot with the camera fixed on a crane to create that dramatic sweep through the air.

'I was aware of the need to get it absolutely right, otherwise I was going to ruin the end of the series. We shot Sam from above a lot during that episode: in our heads, he was on an operating table and we're looking down on him, so this was an extension of that, really. It's an unexpected shot; I wanted to turn the world upside down, then get the Test Card Girl in. All one shot. Also, I didn't want to let the Test Card Girl appear too soon, so we distract you by spinning the camera around, showing the children skipping towards the lens, then reveal her right at the end, looking directly into the lens and turning the audience off with a cheeky smile.'

the operation itself; and green is very clinical and gives everything that hospital feel. That was the link there. I used blue, too, so everything felt colder towards the end, then straight back to the warmer colours for the coda at the end of the final episode.'

Such attention to the details of everything on screen – the reason and motivation behind everything we see – is a hell of a task and one that requires a lot of planning and forethought.

'I had to have my own set of rules: what Sam could see, what he could hear, because otherwise it wouldn't have hung together. There were times when I'd have a fun idea for something but if I couldn't rationalize a complete justification for it within those rules it was out. The graveyard scene in episode eight is a good example. John was thrown by it, looking at the dates on the gravestone, wondering how he could have been born then. John was thrown by it, looking at the death date of his supposed parents and wondering how he could have been twelve in 1950 when he'd been four in 1973. He was convinced they had the gravestone wrong. I had to go through it in my head and talk it through with him. If what Morgan is saying is true and he's not in a coma, then in 1973 he's thirty-five. Work backwards from there … born in 1938 "But I am in a coma, aren't I?" Not in this scene, in this scene you're being told it's all

Top: SJ walking Test Card Girl Harriet Rogers through the final scene of episode eight.

Right: SJ with producer Cameron Roach after a tough day's filming.

Opposite: 'Wot No Breaks?' SJ and Phil Glenister sharing a laugh during a rare break in filming on location.

THERE'S NO PLACE LIKE HOME...

SJ Clarkson loves to fill her frames with detail. One particular thread that has appeared in all of the episodes she directed is *The Wizard of Oz*.

'I should make it clear that *Life On Mars* is not a retold version of *The Wizard of Oz*, but there are elements of similarity which I grasped, particularly as the film was a early favourite of mine, something I watched with awe and wonder. Sam is a man lost and trying to find his way home, meeting lots of new friends on the way. Finally, is it actually better where he came from?

'Most people spotted the rainbow at the end behind Sam and Annie [a version of "Somewhere Over the Rainbow" had already played throughout the scenes following Sam's awakening]. I also used one earlier where he crosses a bridge. The colour palette was a nod to the film as well: everything in the future was washed out and muted before returning to the bright colour of 1973 [in the film the real world was shot in sepia while Oz was in full colour].'

Not just in the final episode, either. Whenever we visited Lost and Found in one of SJ's episodes there were always references on the shelves: yellow bricks; a witches broom; a tin-man constructed from biscuit tins and a funnel; a pair of ruby slippers; a pump for 'Courage' beer with a lion on it was even made by the art department because they knew how much SJ loved sneaking these things in.

The dialogue, too: in the first series Gene Hunt makes a sarcastic phone-call to the 'wonderful Wizard of Oz', and Sam is often referred to as 'Dorothy' when Gene thinks he's being particularly girlie. DCI Frank Morgan's name is itself a big tip of the hat, Frank Morgan being the actor who played the Wizard in the original movie.

'They're subtle, more for our enjoyment than anything else. Claire Parker came up with Morgan's name because she knew my obsession. A lovely touch. I didn't tell the crew about it, just to see if they noticed! I had people coming up to me saying, "how spooky, did you know that Morgan was the actor who played the Wizard of Oz?" *Really*? Wow! What a coincidence!

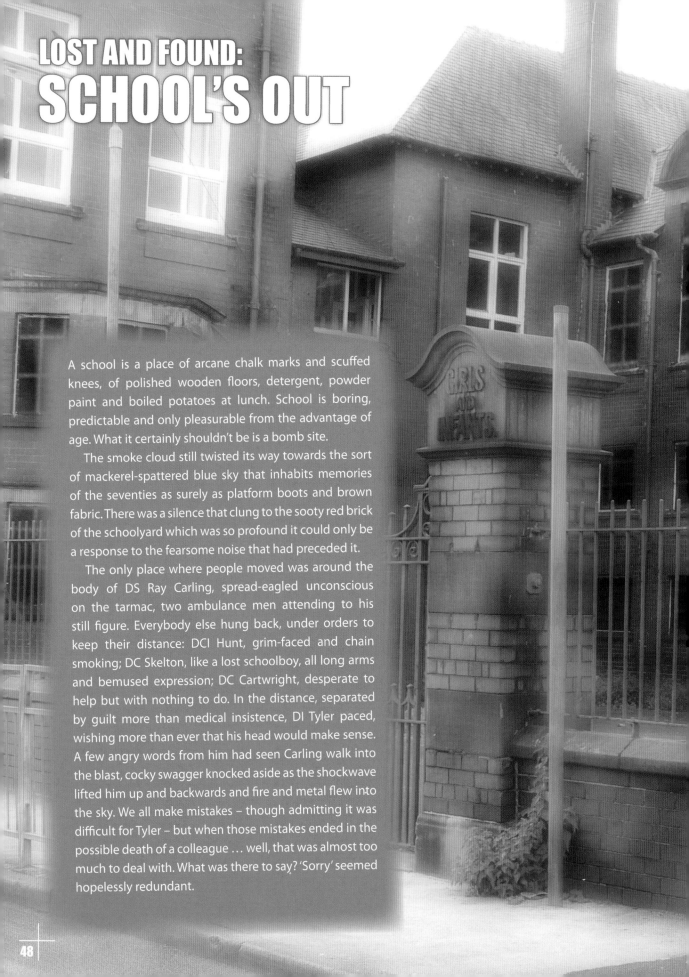

LOST AND FOUND:
SCHOOL'S OUT

A school is a place of arcane chalk marks and scuffed knees, of polished wooden floors, detergent, powder paint and boiled potatoes at lunch. School is boring, predictable and only pleasurable from the advantage of age. What it certainly shouldn't be is a bomb site.

The smoke cloud still twisted its way towards the sort of mackerel-spattered blue sky that inhabits memories of the seventies as surely as platform boots and brown fabric. There was a silence that clung to the sooty red brick of the schoolyard which was so profound it could only be a response to the fearsome noise that had preceded it.

The only place where people moved was around the body of DS Ray Carling, spread-eagled unconscious on the tarmac, two ambulance men attending to his still figure. Everybody else hung back, under orders to keep their distance: DCI Hunt, grim-faced and chain smoking; DC Skelton, like a lost schoolboy, all long arms and bemused expression; DC Cartwright, desperate to help but with nothing to do. In the distance, separated by guilt more than medical insistence, DI Tyler paced, wishing more than ever that his head would make sense. A few angry words from him had seen Carling walk into the blast, cocky swagger knocked aside as the shockwave lifted him up and backwards and fire and metal flew into the sky. We all make mistakes – though admitting it was difficult for Tyler – but when those mistakes ended in the possible death of a colleague … well, that was almost too much to deal with. What was there to say? 'Sorry' seemed hopelessly redundant.

Adams and Thompson hung back. Adams forgot to make notes, Thompson forgot to take pictures. Even when it occurred to them to do so it seemed somehow neither the time nor the place – though they had no doubt that their editor would strongly disagree.

'You think we should talk to him?' Thompson asked, nodding towards Tyler.

'And say what?'

Thompson sighed, turning his camera over awkwardly in his hands, 'I don't know. *Anything*.'

'Go ahead, just don't take it to heart if he chins you one.'

Adams sat down on the kerb as Thompson walked over to Tyler. The writer looked at the crowd of people gathering at the other end of the safety barricade: gossiping housewives, exuberant children – what better way to get a day off school than having someone try and blow it up? They'd be laughing about it for weeks.

His head hurt. The flashes of noise, little gashes in this 'reality' offering glimpses of his body in the future, mangled and bleeding from the crash, were becoming fewer. There had been a time when he would suffer some form of vision every day: the scream of sirens, the tearing of metal, the ghost of music and shouting. Now all was silence. He never thought he could miss it so much.

Thompson stood behind Tyler, shuffling his feet and wondering what to say to the hunched shoulders in front of him.

'He'll be alright,' he said eventually, at a loss for anything more constructive.

The shoulders turned slightly but Tyler didn't face him. 'Know that do you? Utterly convinced of it? As sure of that as your own bloody name?'

Thompson looked over to where the ambulance men were lifting Carling into the back of their vehicle, his body slung on a stretcher. 'No.'

'Doesn't matter. Nothing's sure. The world cheats. Everything you know in your gut is laughed at, torn up and flung back at you.'

What was there to say? 'Can't give up though can you? Got to try and hold on to what you know, otherwise what's left?'

'Nothing,' Tyler muttered, pushing himself to his feet. He glanced at Thompson, red-faced, and walked away.

BUILDING ON THE PAST
DESIGNING SERIES TWO

The design department has to be one of the most bizarre areas of the production office. Weird electronic music bubbles from beneath piles of rough sketches and technical layouts. There are more garish wallpaper off-cuts, sofa coverings and carpet samples than you could pick up if Grace Bros department store was still in business. In the corner a gold-painted plastic shrine is worshipped by piles of vinyl LPs, lampshades and mantelpiece ornaments. The windows have been pasted with large sheets of paper covered in movie screen-grabs: Michael Caine threatens Al Pacino with a shotgun as Gene Hackman chases a hitman in New York. 'It really helps to get the tone across when new directors come in,' says the designer, Matt Gant, about the movie stills. 'It means we're all speaking the same visual language.'

Last year Matt worked as art director alongside designer Brian Sykes. Which means…? 'The art director is basically the designer's right-hand man. It depends on the dynamics within your team what the art director does. I've worked for lots of designers, and my job has been different depending on the skills of each one and which parts of the work they want you to get involved with. Predominantly, you do technical drawings; you draw up the sets and liaise with the construction department to get them built. You do script breakdowns, prop lists, vehicles, graphics, signage – basically anything the art department has to do. It helps the designer to run the department; it frees him up to make more design decisions. Of course you want your art director to be creative as well. I hope I was last year and Tom [Still, Matt's art director on series two] certainly is. You want to be able to leave them to do the design work on one set if you have

This page: A collection of images from the 'shopping trip' taken by the art department and props buyers to hunt out genuine seventies furnishings and fixtures for various sets.

Opposite page: John Simm and Yasmin Bannerman try to keep warm on a very cold morning shoot, while members of the sound department use hairdryers (supplied by the makeup team) to warm up the equipment which won't function in the extreme cold!

to be working on another.'

One might be forgiven for thinking that Matt got promoted in order to give him some rest. As it happens, he has had no such thing.

'We had the luxury of having a bit more time on the first episodes of series two: about nine weeks preparation before we started filming – that's quite a bit for a drama. We had to build all the standing sets, of course [the permanent locations used throughout the series: everything has to be cleared away at the end of filming, so there was the small matter of an entire police department to re-construct], and any incidental sets for those first episodes but you do have a bit more time to be sketching and drawing.' Such luxury couldn't last. 'When we hit block two, we were prepping as they

"The casino in episode one was not at all how I imagined it when I read the script, but it went really well, thanks to the location manager throwing a few ideas into the hat."

were filming. I would be dealing with one director who would be filming episodes while juggling the other directors who were preparing to film theirs. On top of that, I need time to go on recces for locations and so on. You have to find a quick way to have discussions. I've also found it's good not to narrow the location brief too much until you see what the location manager comes back with.

They might find something you hadn't imagined that will work brilliantly. Sometimes the element of chance lends a hand and you can build on a location with dressing, decoration, props or building small pieces of scenery.

'To give an example: the casino in episode one of the second series was not at all how I imagined it when I read the script; but I think it

went really well, which was all down to letting the location manager throw a few ideas into the hat.'

The art department is a busy place. Lots of people lit by the glare of their Apple Mac screens and the terrifying knowledge that everything they're working on was needed *yesterday*.

'As well as the art director and designer you've got a buyer who is responsible for buying props and keeping an eye on the budget. Ron Pritchard is my production buyer and is extremely experienced; he knows at the drop of a hat where to get a prop. I give Ron a list of what we need and he knows if we're better off buying something or if it's more cost affective to hire it from the props store. At the beginning of the series, for example, we went out and bought a lot of furniture that we've used on different sets which was economical. With

> **"It's okay if you've been given a bit of time – you can always come up with something – but you often get that 'rabbit in the headlamps feeling' when you're up against an immediate problem that needs a solution!"**

the prop master, Ron organizes picking things up, dropping them off and keeping track of how long we've had everything for. He also organizes the dressing crew who work with the designer and art director, dressing the sets and then clearing them when finished.

'Then, back in the office we've got another arts assistant, who on this job is predominantly producing lots of graphics, period signage, and running that side of things. He also builds models and any other small jobs that are needed. We've had quite a few runners too who just come on set for a week or two at a time to learn the ropes. They get a lot out of it and are good additions to the team.'

Once things have been dealt with by the design department they move on to the next stage of development.

'It then goes to the construction department which is basically a construction manager, as we don't have a large enough budget to keep painters and carpenters on as full-time staff – we get labour in as and when we need it on a daily rate. Then there are a couple of people on set who make sure everything looks as it should while the unit is filming, working with the camera operator and director to set the scene, as well as a

Left: The Railway Arms set shared space with Sam's flat, so one would have to be dismantled to assemble the other.

stand-by carpenter to do any woodworking jobs that are needed.'

It seems bizarre that filming should require an emergency carpenter to be on hand, but in fact he's an essential member of the crew.

'He helps lay the track for the dolly [movable camera] and is on hand to move bits of scenery, help with props and deal with things that need to be taken apart – taking doors off, that sort of thing. He's a very busy man.'

The countless people behind the scenes who are vital to getting the episode filmed on schedule remain largely unknown to the audience. But there must be times when the pressure gets intense. Has Matt ever suffered from the fear of a blank page? That moment when you can't for the life of you think how to go about something?

'Yes, of course; usually when I've been put on the spot. It's okay if you've been given a bit of time – you can always come up with something – but you often get that "rabbit in the headlamps feeling" when you're up against an immediate problem that needs a solution. You just have to get over it and get on with the job. Also the director usually has a strong idea of how they want it to look so you're facilitating that idea, adding to it, building on it. It's rare you're starting with a completely blank page. Okay, I'm the designer, so I do the set the way I want it to be; but you have to remember the overall vision, otherwise it loses cohesion. You take their idea and make it as strong as you can, adding as much of yourself in there as is relevant.'

The script clearly provides a good deal of inspiration.

'Obviously, that's always there to work from. But then that frequently changes too as filming goes on. Sometimes we will find a location we really want to use and the director will give the go-ahead to alter the script accordingly so it fits. That's nice on this show, you can have a lot of input: if the location isn't pivotal to the story and they think that the new location works just as well then decisions can be made and suddenly you're in a new place.'

Right: Some of the attention to detail put in by the art department is lost when it comes to the final edit. These images show the hospital room (itself a mimic of Sam's flat) used in the Tony Crane sequences from episode one – scenes too indistinct in the broadcast episode to make out any of the detail.

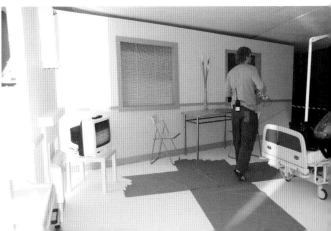

A VISUAL GUIDE BEHIND THE SCENES

This page: *Matt Gant's computer-coloured, pencil sketch of his proposed second series redesigns for the CID office (above) and canteen (below). Ultimately very few changes were made to the sets due to a general decision that Sam Tyler's environment should not have been seen to change between series one and two. The major changes would have been the addition of a translucent partition behind Gene Hunt's office and the addition of a set of swing doors and a pair of windows to the canteen.*

Above: Rear entrance to the BBC Manchester studios, where Life On Mars was shot

Right: The corridor adjoining CID is re-dressed to become the sixth floor where Gene and Sam will have their final showdown with the corrupt Harry Woolf (see middle row left and centre)

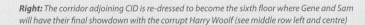

Left: Showing how little space there is between the CID set and studio wall. Floor runners have died here, trapped forever in a jumble of wires and spotlight gels.

Above: One of the few additions to the CID set was the inclusion of a lift. You can see the old CID corridor (sans lift) on the right of the middle row.

Top row: Lost and found – not so scary with the lights on, is it? Note the use of two real brick studio walls at the back. Despite the fact that most of the audience would never notice, all the props used were of the period and frequently changed.

Second row: Sam's room. For which we can only hope he paid no more than ten pence a month, despite its extensive cooking and leisure facilities. Surprisingly, the wallpaper used was one of the most extravagant purchases of the design team as it was genuine vintage paper and extremely expensive. Well, it is beautiful…

Left and bottom row: As was often the case, the CID canteen set was redressed rather nicely to form the background of a sequence for episode six where Maya sings a lovely song to Sam telling him he's dumped. Sadly the scene didn't make it into the transmitted version. Cameron Roach (bottom right, seated) series producer and, for this sequence, director, didn't get cross because he's a professional.

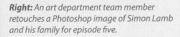

Above left: *Each and every set build requires a considerable amount of research: architectural drawings, pattern samples and sketches to ensure accuracy*

Above right: *Police files are being made up to dress the CID set. This is very historically accurate as people like Gene Hunt used to make up all of their reports too.*

Left: *A notice board in CID: Most of the images are members of the production crew posing as criminals. They do this rather well.*

Right: *An art department team member retouches a Photoshop image of Simon Lamb and his family for episode five.*

Left: *This notice board was used inside the Irish Community Centre in episode three. It has been remounted here so that a 'pick up' shot of Gene tearing a poster off it can be filmed. Pick up shots are often filmed after the fact, either to add more clarification to a scene or simply because a shoot ran out of time.*

Much of the work the art department produces is fine detail dressing that is often missed by viewers. Here we can see stationery for the post office in episode two (right) and manufactured period packaging for Smarties and Mars Bars (below left).

Below: *A detailed model of Sam's hospital room from episode one.*

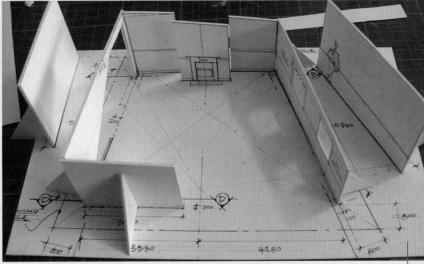

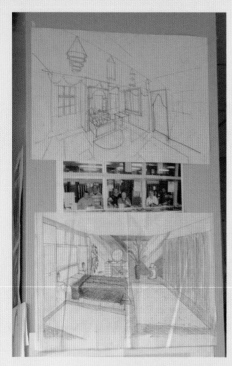

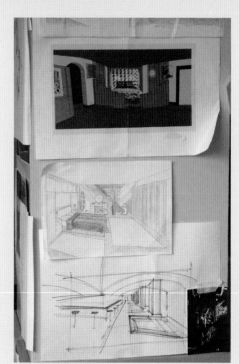

Left and right: Production sketches for various rooms in Roger Twilling's swingers pad from episode four.

Below: Before and after shots of the lounge and then bedroom of the location used for the swingers pad. You will note they kept the lovely zebra print cushions. Beneath the sofa cushions on the left are secreted two pairs of handcuffs, a feather duster and a blow up lady. Just for authenticity.

Top row: *Post Office set for episode two. On the left we can see some jolly rogues from the construction and art department practising for life on 'civvy street' if all the telly work dries up. As well as using some specially manufactured set dressing the post office was bulked out with typewriters and paperwork from the CID office.*

Second row downwards: *Much of the work of the art department on location is concerned with hiding the modern trappings that could end up on screen and spoil the illusion. Often sheets of corrugated iron were draped over shop windows and large period vans parked up to block modern cars from view. Here an electricity sub-station is being barricaded away (above), a line of washing covers a burglar alarm (centre left). Meanwhile the advert for 'Hyde's Anvil Stout' (below), which is also a nice wink to the division Sam is supposed to have hailed from, conceals someone's conservatory.*

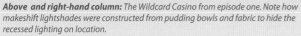

Above and right-hand column: *The Wildcard Casino from episode one. Note how makeshift lightshades were constructed from pudding bowls and fabric to hide the recessed lighting on location.*

Below (left and centre): *Matt Gant dresses a window with some old fashioned signage. Bless him, though, he's printed the 'k' a bit wrong! Nick Beek-Sanders is the camera operator on Life On Mars and Matt obviously thinks he's going to get a pint out of him for getting his name on screen.*

Below (right): *Plastic bins so that the Cortina bumper isn't knackered after a couple of takes of Phil Glenister doing his very best parking.*

Bottom: *Bill posters add more detail to the period location scenes.*

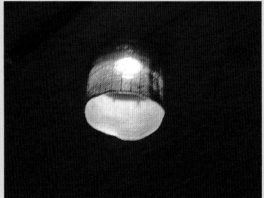

This page: *The record shop location for episode six. As you can see it was a lovely place before the boys moved in with lots of genuine seventies plasterwork all over the rotting floor.*

On location a carpenter and electrician are called in to make sure the place is safe before any filming can begin. All the wiring is checked and someone whacks the walls with a hammer before gleefully declaring it 'safe as bloody houses, that.' In this case the floor was reinforced in order to bear the load of cast, crew, camera and sound equipment.

Right and below: *you can see how this horrible looking dive was turned into … well, a horrible looking dive with records in.*

LOST AND FOUND:
A PINT AND A PROMISE

The Deveraux Pub was not all that popular, for two main reasons. Firstly, the drinks were priced over the odds, and secondly, you're never going to get rich in Deansgate if your target drinker can't pronounce the name over the door. But then the landlord wasn't really much of a one for logic. If he had been, he wouldn't have spent so much money on the carpet around the dance floor: a strip of deep shag that had been scrubbed of drink and fag-ash so often it had forgotten what colour it had been when it had left the dealer. Still, the place had some benefits. Its pretension made it a frequent haunt for lads on a promise in the misguided hope that the lucky lady dripping off their arm would be knocked bandy by the sophistication of padded seats and Engelbert Humperdinck on the jukebox. The rest of the clientele was composed entirely of drinkers who had crossed the threshold by mistake and would move on to a more reasonable bar the minute they had drained their precious beverages.

Adams and Thompson were definitely in the second camp, but the familiar face they spotted at the bar was a fully paid-

'DC Skelton?' Thompson said as he took his wallet back out of his pocket in order to pay a second instalment on his gin and tonic.

The curtain haired detective gave a huge gormless grin. 'Aaaaaay! You're that bloke.'

'Yeah… That's the one,' Thompson replied, his eyes watering as the full force of Skelton's alcoholic breath burned into them. 'What are you up to, then?'

Skelton gestured vaguely over his shoulder. 'On a date. Good looking too…'

Thompson scanned the room. A middle-aged woman was polishing her thick glasses on a chunky red sweater but other than that… Poor Skelton. The woman dropped her glasses and sent empty pint pots and a brimming ashtray flying in her attempt to catch them. 'That her?'

'Yeah … she's a dead ringer for that woman in The Killing of George's Sister.'

'*The Killing of Sister George*? Yeah, now you mention it, she does look a bit like Beryl Reid…'

'You know, the blonde lezza, sexy one.'

'Oh… Right. *Her.*' Thompson breathed a sigh of relief as he spotted a far more attractive and much younger girl behind the red-sweatered woman. Swiftly on the heels of that relief came amazement that Skelton could pull someone so unafflicted by either short-sightedness or visible physical handicap. He must have hidden depths…

'Good film, that,' Chris was saying. 'Well, the lezza bit anyway. I fell asleep during the rest.'

…Or maybe not.

Skelton tried to lift his drinks: two pints of Pernod and Black. 'Get this down her and I'll be

unstoppable … ball-deep by midnight, just you watch.'

'I'd rather not…' Thompson took a mouthful of gin and tonic, trying to hide the involuntary shudder that twisted his lower jaw. 'Best of luck, though.'

'Luck's for losers!' Skelton shouted, turning away from the bar. Two fat tongues of Pernod and Black slopped from the shaken glasses and licked the front of his shirt. 'Bollocks,' he said happily and staggered off towards his table.

Thompson smiled and carried his drink over to where he and Adams were sitting.

'Just bumped into Chris Skelton,' he said, handing Adams a pint of lager. 'He's over there, trying to get a woman to sleep with him.'

Adams glanced over his shoulder and grinned at the sight of the policeman chugging his foul-looking drink down his neck. 'By the time she's finished putting that away she'll think she's sitting with Robert Redford.'

Skelton put his glass down unsteadily and leaned forward in his seat. His date, perhaps mistaking the glazed look in his eyes for something approaching lust, leaned forward too, happy to offer her lips should he wish to make use of them. In this position she received the full technicolor contents of Skelton's guts as he threw them up all over her. She jumped to her feet, caught her heel in a slick of vomit and landed on her backside, with Skelton staring wide-eyed in abject horror.

Adams and Thompson looked at one another, put down their drinks and made their way towards the exit.

SPEAKING LIKE A COMPLETE HUNT
VOLUME TWO

Gene Hunt: a modern-day Oscar Wilde, always ready with a choice *bon mot* or witticism. There are few situations in which the Shakespeare of seventies policing cannot turn his leviathan of a mind to the careful construction of a sentence that does precisely what he needs it to with clarity and intelligence. Who can forget, for example, that moment of sheer unadulterated poetry in the final episode of the series when, forced to take a short cut through a tight alleyway festooned with laundry in the Cortina, he suggests that the two ladies fixing their smalls to the line mind their toes. *'Get out the way, you bitches!'* he shouts, adding, by way of encouragement, *'Go on a diet, you lardy cow!'* to the more amply framed of the two.

There is more to Gene than the straight-forward insult, of course. In episode three, when Sam suggests that their current case may have nothing to do with the Irish community, he proves himself a master of both current affairs and sarcasm: *'And maybe Enoch Powell is throwing one up Shirley Bassey. Let me know when you're back living in the real world, Tyler.'*

There are certainly times when plucky young Tyler faces the sharp edge of Gene's tongue, here in episode two for instance:

> *Sam: I'm following my instincts*
> *Gene: well, I should charge your instincts with wasting police time.*

Here and there, though, amidst the barrage of jibes at Sam's expense, the discerning ear can detect a note of gruff affection that not even Gene can hide; as when, deriding Sam for claiming to love his girlfriend in episode six, he calls him a *'great, soft, sissy, girlie, nancy, French, bender, Man United-supporting poof!'*

Still, despite his obvious genius with description there are times when DCI Hunt's grasp of the English language proves a little slippery, in episode two for instance:

Gene: Right, Scotland Yard are sending up some sort of kleptomanic.
Sam: Cryptographer.
Gene: Whatever.

Most of the time no-one is spared from his sharp edge of his tongue – not his team, not Gene himself, and certainly not those foolish enough to find themselves on the wrong side of the law. And as far as Gene is concerned, there is no sensitivity that can't be trampled on, and no subject that's taboo…To a suspect protesting that his multiple bank accounts are legitimate (from episode six):

'You've got fingers in more pies than a leper on a cookery course.'

To a grieving mother in episode four whose teenage son has been convicted (wrongly, as it happens) of murder:

'…if there's a hell, he is going there to be poked up the arse with sharp fiery sticks, forever and ever amen!'

On drugs (episode six again):

'What's the point? They make you forget, they make you talk funny, they make you see things that aren't there. My Gran got all that for free when she had a stroke.'

On the perils that await him after he himself has been framed for a revenge killing in episode seven:

'You're not the one that's going to have to knit himself a new arsehole after twenty-five years of aggressive male affection in prison showers!'

But of all the classic Hunt-speak with which the series sparkles, there is one – from episode six – that stands alone, at least in terms of the number of different minorities it is possible to outrage within a single statement:

Gene: All the dealers are so scared we're more likely to get Helen Keller to talk. The Paki in a coma is about as lively as Liberace's dick when he's looking at a woman. All in all, this investigation's going at the speed of a spastic in a magnet factory...

SAM is just staring at him, appalled at the sheer volume of abuse in such a short space of time

Gene: What?

Sam: I think you might have left out the Jews...?

PLASTIC FANTASTIC
Behind the scenes with Hot Animation

'This is a box, a magical box, playing a magical tune. But inside this box there lies a surprise. Do you know who's in it today?'

Anything can happen in *Life On Mars*: bewhiskered professors from the Open University talk to us with alarming regularity, radios blast out the persistent beeps and wheezes of hospital equipment, the Test Card Girl offers advice and scares in equal measure, her clown dragged softly behind her. Still, the opening of the fifth episode of the second series offered one of the most bizarre and enjoyable pieces of surrealism of the show's entire run. On a cluttered police desk stands a familiar music box out of which – as the jingle jangle of its tinny tune plays – rises an even more familiar figure: Sam Tyler has been reborn in the style of *Camberwick Green*!

Originally written and produced by Gordon Murray with animation by Bob Bura and John Hardwick, *Camberwick Green* appeared on our screens in 1966 and was the first of Murray's Trumptonshire sequence (*Trumpton* and *Chigley* would follow over the next few years). A staple memory from many childhoods, the combination of crackly nostalgia and the sight of a Plasticine Gene Hunt kicking in a nonce (who waved sportingly at the screen when the narrator mentioned him) turned what was only a brief sequence into of the most talked-about scenes from the series. In fact a portion of it was used as the first 'teaser' trailer for the new series by the BBC.

To realize Matthew Graham's idea, Kudos turned to Hot Animation, one of the UK's leading animation companies, most famously responsible for Bob the Builder. The puppets were designed and animated by Paul Couvella, while the director of the sequence was Geoff Walker.

'Most of what we do is children's programming,' says Geoff, 'so it was fun to be able to do an adult programme. The fact that we were able to pull it off beyond even Kudos's expectations made it even better!

'To begin with, we had a meeting with Kudos and went through the little piece of script they would show us. They were obviously very secretive

> **"Most of what we do are children's shows so it was fun to be able to do an adult programme. The fact that we were able to pull it off beyond even Kudos's expectations made it even better!"**

Above: Foam-core board and cardboard is used to create a model of the set to show camera angles and scales. *Right:* Using the card model as a guide, the set builder constructs the actual set using fibreboard and a textured paint.

about what was going to happen in the second series so we just had the first page of that episode. We discussed *Camberwick Green*, the look and atmosphere of that and then how we could try and carry over the whole feel of *Life On Mars* into that 'world'. We went away and drew up some designs to give them an idea of the style of the sets, the look of the characters, the lighting and so on and then sat down to watch a lot of *Camberwick Green*.'

One of the main challenges for them must have been creating recognisable versions of Sam Tyler and Gene Hunt, given the limited facial characteristics of the *Camberwick Green* puppets.

'They are just round heads! It's very difficult to strip something down to that level. Paul studied photos of John Simm and Phil Glenister to try and get elements of their faces into the design. It's a difficult process: simplifying the face but keeping the essence of the character.'

A caricature, effectively – with a fag in the gob for Gene and some corking eyebrows for Sam that could feature in a show of their own.

'The costumes were very authentic, too: some of them were done with old seventies clothes that we got from charity shops, cutting up the fabric and re-stitching them into smaller versions.'

That sort of attention to detail even went into the construction of the stage on which the music box was filmed: 'The majority of the dressing we used on the desk,

the police files and stuff, were taken from the *Life On Mars* prop store, things that had been used in the series.'

Geoff's attention to detail didn't just extend to authentic costumes and props. There was also a great determination to mirror the look of the old-fashioned techniques of animation in the sixties.

'It was difficult, because watching *Camberwick Green* now you are struck by how basic the animation is. So we had to mimic it enough to create the same feel, but also update it, because if we'd stuck with the animation style slavishly it would have looked pretty bad. When you're a child, you fill in the gaps in your head. Look at *Captain Pugwash* for instance [another classic series produced by Gordon Murray with stories from John Ryan, the character's creator]. Your memory tells you it was full animation with the characters moving around and interacting; but actually it's just still pictures with their mouths moving. As a child you fill in those gaps. So, we tweaked it, made it smoother, but kept the movements simple.'

Like Gene simultaneously smacking the nonce with a dustbin lid while kicking him in the gut.

'Yeah, they would never have attempted something like that back then! Much too complicated.'

The other element of historical accuracy was the construction of the puppets themselves. 'They were Ping Pong balls and wire, really basic. These days, a lot of puppets are highly engineered: ball and socket joints, lots of high-level mechanics; but we wanted to stick to the old methods. Most of us made puppets like that when we were at college, its an easy and quick way of getting a puppet up and running without spending weeks checking the tension on a ball and socket joint. It makes the movements jerkier though, pretty crude stuff – not as lithe as Bob the Builder!'

Animation is notoriously slow work – as director SJ Clarkson mentioned. How long did it take to film the whole thing?

'We allotted three days but it took five in the end … five days for forty seconds!'

Now *that's* patience.

'The thing is, a lot of animators *aren't* very patient, that's the weird thing with this profession. You carry on because you're so determined to achieve the end result; it's a funny contradiction and tension in the filming process. Impatience is what drives you to get it done.'

The process of directing animation is obviously very different from working in live action filming.

'It's the same language but a whole different ball game: I haven't done any live action work but it seems to me that the important

*Left: Detail is hand painted on the arches. **Bottom two:** The final set on the animation stage.*

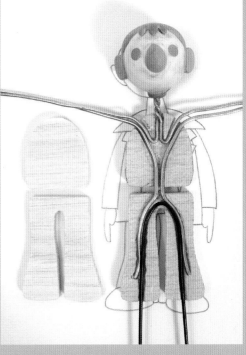

This page: From full-scale sketch to wire-and-wood skeleton, complete with ping-pong ball head, Camberwick Green Sam comes together.

For flexibility, Sam's arms, neck and lower legs are constructed using foam, allowing a wider range of expression.

Sam is then clothed with a costume constructed of genuine vintage 1970s fabrics. Note the detail of the St Christopher!

STOP-MOTION ANIMATION

Stop-motion is an animation technique that has been in use since the early part of the twentieth century. Its time-consuming but effective trick is to shoot a long sequence of single frames of an inanimate object, moving that object ever so slightly between shots. By then running those shots together as a continuous piece of footage the appearance of motion is created. It has been used to create everything from Tony Hart's *Morph* to, well … *Camberwick Green*.

Willis O'Brien, the pioneering model maker who used stop-motion techniques to bring the 1933 *King Kong* movie to the screen inspired a surge of such methods in Hollywood. One man would go on to make the method his own: Ray Harryhausen. He used stop-motion extensively in his long list of credits, animating fighting skeletons in *Jason and the Argonauts*, the insect-like Selenites in the H.G. Wells adaptation *First Men in the Moon* and a whole host of creatures (centaurs, sabre-tooth tigers and even a giant walrus) for his trilogy of *Sinbad* movies.

Today, extensive use of computer generated effects has supplanted stop-motion as the popular method of creating such fantasies, despite the arguably greater 'depth' and texture that stop-motion still offers. There are still some popular examples to be found: Tim Burton is a great fan of the method having used it for *The Nightmare Before Christmas*, *James and the Giant Peach* and *The Corpse Bride*. Aardman Animation use the technique too for their highly popular *Creature Comforts* series as well as the movie *Chicken Run* and the various adventures of *Wallace and Gromit*.

thing is how you get on with the actors, how you get your performance. In animation you're getting a performance from an animator by telling them precisely what you want them to do. I imagine live action exists as a compromise between the director and the artistes whereas our artistes are made of balsa wood, wire and Plasticine.'

One thing that differed from the original *Camberwick Green* was the voice of the narrator. Actor Brian Cant narrated all three of Gordon Murray's Trumptonshire shows, in addition to being a regular presenter of *Play School* for eighteen years. When *Camberwick Green* was briefly revived to advertise a brand of porridge it was voiced by comedian Charlie Higson. The substitution in the case of *Life On Mars* came about purely because the 'stand-in' went down so well.

'It was Brian Little who did the voice; he's one of the directors here [indeed, one of the co-founders of Hot Animation]. You have to animate to a soundtrack, so that you know how long each shot needs to be, where the action is placed, that sort of thing; so we got him do what is called a guide track. We sent that along to Kudos with the footage and they really liked him, so he had to go into a recording studio and do a proper version for them. Ironically, he has actually worked with Brian Cant; he's been in the industry for thirty years.'

And what a dedicated industry it is. These days when so much animation is produced using computer generated effects, the skills and talents of people like Hot Animation are unquestionably impressive. How did Geoff get into the business in the first place?

'As a kid, I was always drawing, and my imagination was influenced by all the cartoons that were on at the time. It was an interest that was always bubbling under the surface and when I did a degree in graphic design, there was an animation strand that I could opt for. I tried it, just to see how it went, and loved it. To get to the point when I was able to consider actually making a go of it as a career was unbelievable. I worked as an animator first, working on *Old Bear Stories*, which won a BAFTA; *Bob the Builder*, of course; and *El Nombre*, which was a *Zorro* pastiche about Mexican gerbils. I became a director on that and have done both since. I love animating and directing equally, to be honest, so my ideal job would be to be left in a room on my own, make it all up and be paid handsomely for it!'

This page: *Creating the Camberwick Green Gene Hunt, showing the constant reference to the original drawings, the patterns used to construct the costume and the detail added to the final model.*

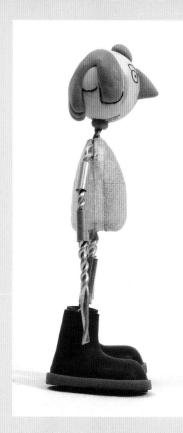

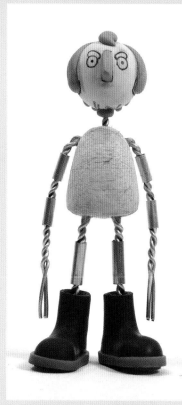

Above: Showing the framework of The Nonce's skeleton and chest, prior to clothing.

Below: Adding clothing, and finally, some detail such as the glasses (complete with sticking plaster on the bridge) and stubble.

Above and far left: Using photographs of the CID set and props supplied by the Life On Mars art department, the animators were able to recreate a desk, complete with pornography, police files and cigarettes.

Left and below: The finished figures on the lit animation stage.

LOST AND FOUND:
A BUMP IN THE ROAD

Detective Constable Annie Cartwright stood at the front counter with the same slightly unconfident manner she often had about her. A strong woman, yes; but aware that that made her a bump in the road of seventies misogyny and therefore a target. Sometimes, she thought, it can be better to keep one's head down. You don't get anywhere by bucking the system in one riotous shout – progression could be found more successfully on the quiet path, especially if – like her – the idea of confrontation made your pulse race and nerves choked your voice in your throat. She would get ahead in the end; but only if she played the game a little.

'How long do you think it'll be?'

The librarian glanced over his shoulder and carried on flicking through the paperwork in front of him. 'Someone's using it. I don't know, do I?'

Annie sighed and glanced over towards the microfiche reader. The man scrolling through old newspapers on the lit-up screen seemed vaguely familiar.

'I'll see how long he's going to be.' She strolled over, ignoring the obvious irritation of the librarian, and stood at Adams' shoulder.

'Oh,' she said, 'it's you.'

He looked up from his reading and smiled. 'Hello.' He had no idea what else to say, not sure what she might want him for. 'Can I help?' he asked eventually.

'You could hurry up a bit, I need to check something.' She nodded at the screen.

'Oh … right, yeah.' He stood up, 'Help yourself, I can go back on when you've done. No rush.'

'They'll need to change the roll,' she replied. 'I need this time last year.'

'You're in luck, then.' He pointed at the date on the screen. 'That's what I was looking at.'

Annie looked at the front page of the newspaper on the screen: 'FOURTEEN YEAR OLD FOUND BRUTALLY ATTACKED' the headline announced.

Adams shrugged. 'After the radio broadcast, I thought it best to brush up on it, y'know?'

Annie nodded. A man's family kidnapped by 'persons unknown', who were seeking justice over what they saw as the department's mishandling of the case in front of her. Things were, understandably, tense. And the last person she wished to discuss it with – most particularly because of the churning in her gut that told her that maybe mistakes *had* been made – was a journalist.

'Horrible,' he said, more out of an attempt to say the right thing than from real concern, she felt.

'Yes, it was.' His presence at her shoulder was beginning to irritate; she couldn't work with him stood over her. She glanced up but he wasn't even looking at the screen, just staring into space. 'Are you alright?' she asked.

He looked confused. 'Yeah … just, I don't know. I've been feeling a bit of out of it lately.'

'Probably lead poisoning from licking your reporter's pencil,' she replied.

He smiled. 'That's the only thing that makes me feel better.' He looked at the screen. 'Does Hunt know you're looking into this?'

A surge of guilt made her answer less controlled than she might have liked. 'Of course.'

'Didn't think so.' He smiled again. 'Watch your back, then.'

She opened her mouth to speak but he shook his head, 'Don't worry. I'm not in the mood for reporting today. I won't mention you were here.' He made to walk off, that vague and unsettled look creeping back over his face again as he glanced out of the library window. He paused and turned back to her. 'Are you happy?' he asked.

She stared at him for a second, 'That's a funny question.'

'Depends entirely on your answer. A woman stuck in the wrong time and place, forever pushed aside, insulted, patronised … how do you do it?'

Annie thought for a moment. 'I just get on with it. What else can you do? You get on with your job, do the best you can; work hard, take it on the chin and hope that one day you'll fit in.'

He thought about this for a moment, then nodded and carried on walking out.

Annie turned back to the microfiche and began to read.

A DAY IN THE LIFE
Filming the Show

There is a tendency to imagine that filming is all non-stop excitement, bustle and glamour, with people shouting 'Marks, everyone!' and 'Action!' and 'Cut!' This is very far removed from the reality, as *Life On Mars: The Official Companion* found out. The fact is that it requires an almost zen-like ability to rise above distractions, and the patience of the proverbial saint, as our light-hearted diary account of one morning's shooting reveals.

8.00 A.M.

It's early morning and the sun's already baking our backs crisper than the bacon being flipped on the hissing griddles of the catering van. England's in the grip of a heat wave and the call sheets sent out to cast and crew with details of the location and time of filming come with health advice: sun-block and gallons of water are the order of the day – the production office doesn't want any fatalities.

We're here to watch a few scenes for the sixth episode of the second series being filmed. Lee is snapping photos to use in the book and I'm trying to forge some kind of sunshade from my notebook and generally keep out of the way. The episode opens in a back-street record shop owned by a pair of Ugandan Asian brothers – one of whom will be found flat on his back with a gunshot wound in his chest a couple of minutes in. Before the location manager, Luc Webster, and his team

Above: *Before and After shots of the record shop location in Rusholme.*

found the site and flagged it for use it was a decrepit corner shop ripe for wrecking. In a few days' time it will be again. The landlord has his eye on gutting the building and converting it into a couple of flats. For now, though, it exists in fictional grace, reliving the seventies for a few days before the sledgehammers fall.

The day before, we had poked around while designer Matt Gant and his team put the finishing touches to the set dressing that would hide the truth of the place. It felt a little awkward just standing and observing while all around us everyone else was hammering, taping and ferrying tea chests of props to and fro, so we mucked in to ensure that all the LPs on display in the record store racks were from 1973 or earlier. Bucks Fizz is concealed by Bowie (pre-*Aladdin Sane* era, naturally) while Hendrix blocks the anachronistic pizzazz of Dollar with his beads and bandana. Even the most eagle-eyed viewer will find nothing to break the illusion: not on our watch.

There's a hint of *Mission Impossible* in the speed and casual professionalism with which the team carries off the transformation. One large truck pulls up, a handful of men pile out and within a couple of hours the disguise is complete, just waiting to fool people. We half-expect the corrupt *el Presidente* of some obscure Latin country to be dragged in unconscious, woken up and bamboozled into thinking he's shot a man in a record shop; and unless he releases the blueprints for his death ray his career in politics is over… We tug experimentally at Matt Gant's face to see if it's a rubber mask, but that makes him angry so we stop. We conclude that he is who he appears to be.

8.30 A.M.

Here and now in the large car park where the filming unit is making its base we chew on bacon rolls while watching the crew come to life. Some are still getting things organized, talking on mobiles, passing sheets of paper – no breakfast for them. The actors have formed a queue at the catering van, plates of 'full English' ferried back to the bus which they use as a comfortable refuge to drown early morning sleepiness in bacon fat and coffee, waiting for the call.

9.00 A.M.

After another half hour or so, everyone is approaching readiness and we stroll down the road to the location. We're not the only spectators: you don't put a film crew in the middle of a residential street and expect to remain unnoticed. Taped barriers keep people away from the camera sight lines as crowds gather to see 'them off of the telly'.

Possessing a notebook earmarks me as an insider who is privy to the secrets of the show. Everyone wants to know how the series will end. *Everyone.* When I waffle evasively about being a writer and nothing to do with the film crew really, I'm offered a constant stream of anecdotes from the seventies as reproof. Everyone wants to tell me what they were doing at the time. One man in particular relishes the opportunity to tell me of an acquaintance in the police force who once interrogated a suspected child abuser with a broken desk lamp. It's difficult to know what to say. 'Things were simpler back then…' he announces, wistfully, as I try and make my escape to the refreshments table.

9.30 A.M.

Due to the extreme heat – a summer not unlike the ones that seem to feature in everyone's anecdotes – gallons of water and orange squash are being poured and consumed. Drinking also gives you something to do, as filming is an incredibly slow process. Each shot

JUST A DESK JOB

Picture the scene: you arrive to dress the location set due to be used for filming the following day; you unload two heavy old filing cabinets, boxes of vinyl records and shop equipment; you've painted the outside of the building with new signs. Then you notice that the wonderful period desk you've just heaved off the truck is about three inches too wide to fit in either of the two doorways in to the property.

Bugger.

So, what happens in this situation? You take the desk apart! And it's at times like this that on-set carpenters come in handy with a power drill and a strong forearm.

The photos above show how a straightforward moving job can turn into an arduous task that simply *has* to be done for the set to be ready for filming.

takes an age to set up: so many things to check, so many angles, lighting conditions… Then, once everything is in place and the call goes out to halt the traffic in preparation for some high-grade Phil Glenister stunt driving, a plane flies overhead and everyone sags. And waits… And waits some more.

9.35 A.M.

Finally the plane clears, but the traffic is getting antsy: someone is late for work and needs to get through. So the cars are allowed past quickly before the road is closed for a second time and the signal given to Phil, who by now is practically chewing the steering wheel with tension as he prepares to swing the Cortina round a corner and into some plastic bins. The car revs, wheels screech, bumper hits plastic bin and … someone in one of the nearby terraced houses decides that this would be the perfect moment to shout at the top of his voice. The director sighs and wishes he could send out the order to have the intrusive resident assassinated by the secret Kudos hit squad, a crack team of Ninja-style psychos who live for the spilling of blood. He is reminded that no such squad exists and that if he wants the man taken out he'll have to do it himself. This is not good news. Best thing is to reset the bins and try again.

9.45 A.M.

Phil's teeth are prised from the leatherette steering wheel cover and the boiling actor goes back to his start position. At the start of the day the cast made a valiant bid to shoot the scene

Top: Make-up supervisor Debbie Salmon pops a little slap on John Simm.

Bottom: The director and script supervisors watch over the action on a monitor.

Opposite: The shot everyone is trying to get in the can.

without camel coats, leather jackets or other items of wardrobe torture. Unfortunately, due to continuity reasons, the request has been denied. If we don't get this scene soon, Phil, John, Marshal, Dean and Liz will have lost several stone between them, and will have to be force-fed chips in order to look like the same actors they were at the start of the series.

10.00 A.M.

The car is sent back to the start position and the process starts anew. Everything's checked, cued up, poked at, stripped down, polished, correctly lit, taken out for dinner and given a proposal of marriage. The most difficult part of all this for the actors is maintaining focus. Okay, so in this scenario it boils down to slamming some bins with a car: but it could so easily have been something requiring some major acting weight, maintaining a level of intensity, preparation and performance despite the fact that it could take all morning to get a few minutes done. Now that's *hard*.

10.30 A.M.

Someone has decided to up the ante by stripping off and pressing himself against the upstairs window of his flat. The most rewarding part of this is how *little* it moves the entire crew. A few glances in his direction and then it's back to business, with a nude man shuffling awkwardly back off his windowsill feeling insecure and physically inadequate. It's not even as if he can blame the cold. His antics bother us not one jot as the car comes screaming around the corner again and gives those design-department bins what for.

This time it works. The gang leap out of the car and head towards the shop, clutching bacon and egg butties (which, for continuity reasons, they've been unable to sample throughout this scene) and then collapse from heat exhaustion as the camera stops rolling.

11.00 A.M.

Once the actors have been resuscitated they celebrate their success with plastic cups of orange squash and a glance at the day's papers. All except for John Simm, that is, who hasn't got time for such leisure pursuits as doing *The Times* crossword or keeping his eyes peeled for a stray Bourbon biscuit. He climbs into the back of his car to try and learn precisely what he is expected to say in the next few scenes. When you're in every single scene and you play a man with a bit of a mouth on him, the amount of dialogue you have to get through your head is unbelievable.

12.00 P.M.

One by one, people sit under a parasol in front of the makeup team and have the effects of the unrelenting heat mopped from perspiring brows and hidden beneath foundation. The sun continues to burn. Four hours have passed and all that's completed is a shot of a car hitting some bins. A small group of technicians make a break for freedom but are captured and dragged back, forced to fix the lights inside the record shop so that the next scene can be filmed. Sam Tyler's not the only one trapped here.

1.00 P.M.

There's not enough room for intrusive authors or book designers in such a small set so Lee and I decide to make a run for it, back to Manchester City Centre and the air-conditioned glory of production offices and coffee bars. Never has a fan and a Cappuccino felt so heavenly. The past, we conclude, is an interesting place, but all in all, we'd prefer not to live in it.

WHEN IS SAM TYLER NOT JOHN SIMM?

When he's floor runner and stand-in Mark Ashmore!

The production team brought Mark in for the second series to help set up lighting and camera positions without using John Simm, providing him with extra time to concentrate on his scripts. Mark was chosen because his height, build and skin tone closely match that of John's. Mark was frequently called on to provide his hands for close-up shots too. When not in front of the camera, Mark often spent time assisting the crew in various roles (including being nice to book writers and designers) and even filmed the Tufty sequences seen in the DVD extras.

LOST AND FOUND:
ACCIDENT WAITING TO HAPPEN

Hospitals smell bad. The bleach and floor wax never quite cover the vomit, ointment and death. It's the essential contradiction of such institutions that they exist to make people well, yet their atmosphere is such that they depress anyone forced to be there. Not least the staff.

Thompson was trapped firmly against one side of a corridor, the motorized floor cleaner having thrust itself against the skirting the minute he switched it on and refused to move. He nodded at occasional passers-by as the engine roared and wrestled with the thing when he thought nobody would notice. Eventually he switched it off: it moved easily enough then, but he was terrified that the moment he turned it back on again he'd be thrown against the opposite wall. Was he to be stuck in this piece of corridor forever?

'What you doin' 'ere then?' said a voice behind him. Thompson froze, trying to remember his cover story.

He turned around. 'I am come from my homelands for make sweet floors!' he said in what he hoped was a passable foreign accent.

It was DC Ray Carling. 'Well, stop sniffing the wax then,' he said. 'It makes you talk like a twat.'

'I didn't know it was you,' Thompson whispered. 'I'm under cover.'

Carling sneered. 'Undercover my arse, they finally kicked you off the paper.'

Thompson looked around nervously. 'No, seriously; we're doing an article on the poor treatment of patients.'

'Poor treatment?' Carling replied as a nurse walked past. 'When you have girls like that wandering about?' He raised his voice. 'You could give me a bed wash any day, love!' The nurse ignored him but he chuckled as if she had answered him, happy to flirt on his own.

'What brings you here?' Thompson asked, happy to change the subject. 'Nobody ill, I hope?'

Carling grimaced. 'Babysitting a Paki in a coma. One of Tyler's time-wasters.'

'Not keeping much of an eye on him, are you?'

Carling gave him a cold stare. 'I was bored, I fancied a drink. He's not going anywhere, is he?

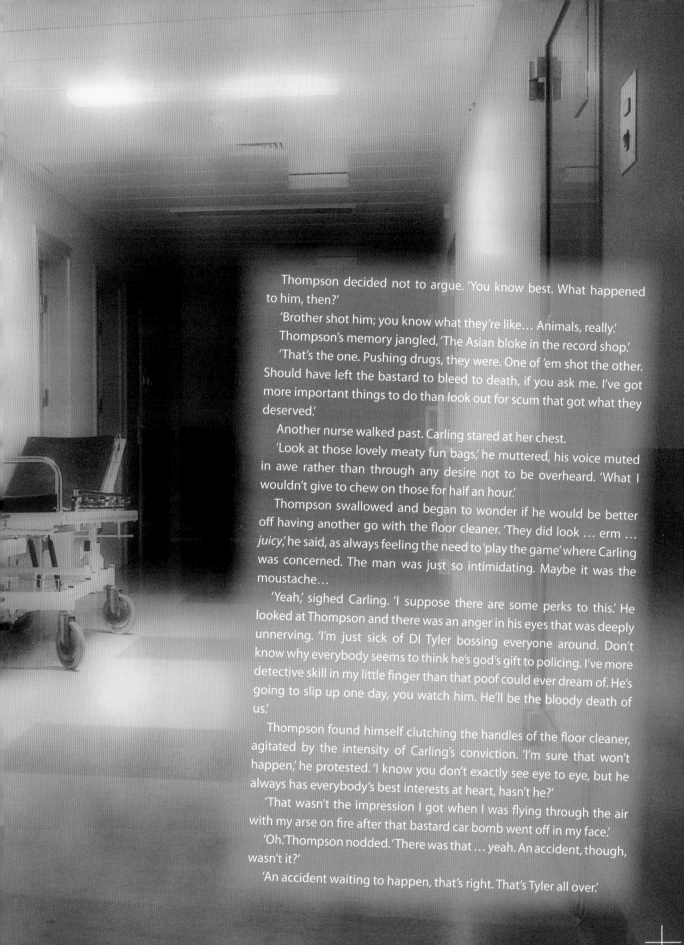

Thompson decided not to argue. 'You know best. What happened to him, then?'

'Brother shot him; you know what they're like… Animals, really.'

Thompson's memory jangled, 'The Asian bloke in the record shop.'

'That's the one. Pushing drugs, they were. One of 'em shot the other. Should have left the bastard to bleed to death, if you ask me. I've got more important things to do than look out for scum that got what they deserved.'

Another nurse walked past. Carling stared at her chest.

'Look at those lovely meaty fun bags,' he muttered, his voice muted in awe rather than through any desire not to be overheard. 'What I wouldn't give to chew on those for half an hour.'

Thompson swallowed and began to wonder if he would be better off having another go with the floor cleaner. 'They did look … erm … *juicy*,' he said, as always feeling the need to 'play the game' where Carling was concerned. The man was just so intimidating. Maybe it was the moustache…

'Yeah,' sighed Carling. 'I suppose there are some perks to this.' He looked at Thompson and there was an anger in his eyes that was deeply unnerving. 'I'm just sick of DI Tyler bossing everyone around. Don't know why everybody seems to think he's god's gift to policing. I've more detective skill in my little finger than that poof could ever dream of. He's going to slip up one day, you watch him. He'll be the bloody death of us.'

Thompson found himself clutching the handles of the floor cleaner, agitated by the intensity of Carling's conviction. 'I'm sure that won't happen,' he protested. 'I know you don't exactly see eye to eye, but he always has everybody's best interests at heart, hasn't he?'

'That wasn't the impression I got when I was flying through the air with my arse on fire after that bastard car bomb went off in my face.'

'Oh.' Thompson nodded. 'There was that … yeah. An accident, though, wasn't it?'

'An accident waiting to happen, that's right. That's Tyler all over.'

THE MAN BEHIND THE CURTAIN
Ralph Brown – aka Frank Morgan

Built on the backs of cotton mills, Hyde is a one-time Cheshire town that now falls under the borough of Greater Manchester. Its early fame as home to the world's best water polo team (the Hyde Seals won the world championship from 1904 to 1906) has been overshadowed somewhat by its association with Britain's most prolific serial killer, Harold Shipman, who had his surgery there; not to mention earlier residents Ian Brady and Myra Hindley, perpetrators of the notorious Moors Murders. Mingle with that chequered past a mental association with Dr Jekyll's alter ego Mr Hyde, that embodiment of the darkest elements of our psyches, and you have a rather eerie-sounding town for Sam Tyler to hail from within the fictional world of *Life On Mars*. From the first episode of the second series onwards he is contacted by a mysterious caller on the end of his telephone who seems to know a great deal about Sam and his condition. When we finally get to meet that man,

DCI Frank Morgan, in the last two episodes of the show, it is with the knowledge that this is a character who will blow the world of Sam Tyler apart.

The actor who plays Morgan, Ralph Brown, is immediately recognizable from a long history of big screen roles. As Danny – 'the purveyor of rare herbs and prescribed chemicals' in *Withnail and I* – he showed the world how to fashion a Camberwell Carrot;

in *Alien³* he gave Lance Henriksen a sound thrashing with a length of pipe which made us like his character a touch more; he even taught the young Anakin Skywalker how to fly in *Star Wars: Episode I – The Phantom Menace*. All this from a man who originally trained as a lawyer. What made him change direction?

'The joke answer is that I foresaw large amounts of arse-licking ahead in order to become a silk, so I chose to be an actor instead. In fact I went up to the Edinburgh Festival at the end of my first year at LSE (London School of Economics) with The National Student Theatre Company after auditioning in London. Everyone else in the cast was at drama school. When they asked me what I would do after university I said, "barrister". When I asked *them* they said "actor". Believe it or not, it had never occurred to me that one could choose acting as a job before that point. For me it was a pastime, an extra-curricular choice like football or chess. Not a job! So I had an epiphany, if you like. I'd have been a good barrister, and I suppose I still could be. My mind works in that way, I think.'

Given the consistency with which he appears on our screens it seems doubtful that he'll need to rethink careers. He is also working proof that attending drama school isn't necessarily a prerequisite for success. 'After three years at LSE I didn't really want to carry on being a student. Of anything. It hasn't hindered me, or many other actors, to have no formal training.'

Most of Ralph's work has been for the screen. 'I prefer going to the cinema rather than the theatre. I prefer films to plays. I think I'm better at screen acting than stage acting. And … it pays better!'

Still, unlike many actors working in film and television he seems to have very successfully avoided being typecast. That alone makes him a rarity. How has he managed to keep his credits so diverse? '*Withnail and I*. Which came from the casting director, the late, great Mary Selway, being desperate, and remembering an actor she'd seen at the Royal Court Theatre playing six different roles – including Robert Maxwell and a striking miner from Rotherham – in a play called *Deadlines*. That was me. Somehow I have managed to transfer my ear for accents and desire to be camouflaged into a career. But as a youth I was obsessed

> **"I was going to call my autobiography 'Acting Not Required', because I always felt that casting directors didn't know who I was, so they never quite knew how to cast me."**

by John Hurt and his ability to transform himself. I foolishly thought that acting was transformation, then watched as my contemporaries like Hugh Grant stuck to the one thing that worked and made millions. I was going to call my autobiography "Acting Not Required", because I always felt that casting directors didn't know who I was, so they never quite knew how to cast me. Can't blame them, because I'm not sure myself. I always felt I could do anything, which is clearly not true, but I do try and stretch myself all the time. I'd get bored just being me – whoever that is!'

All of which begs the question of whether there is a particular type of part he would like to play that has eluded him thus far.

'A lead part would be nice!'

Outside of acting Ralph has also had success as a writer. He won several writing awards for his play *Sanctuary* (which has been performed both in the UK and in the US). *New Years Day*, a film

about two survivors of an avalanche which he wrote in 2001, was voted the best film at the Raindance Film Festival that year. 'I have three screenplays awaiting production but I've got to the stage where *I'm* going to direct them, or no-one is. Making films in the UK is so very hard. Also, my oldest collaborator, Paulette Randall, who directed *Sanctuary*, wants me to write another play for her. We'll see.'

Working as an actor must have helped when it came to scriptwriting?

'Absolutely; you develop an inbuilt bullshit-detector for bad dialogue, which is almost the first rule of writing. Actors always write great dialogue; they have problems with structure, usually.'

Has the experience made him even more analytical with scripts he receives?

'I've had to develop a number of ways to approach scripts. One – as an actor; with total enthusiasm. Get inside the character. *Enjoy*

> "I don't like rude people, especially if they're racist, but Gene Hunt makes a great TV character. He only works though through the prism of John Simm – who is us."

it. Become immersed in the story immediately, uncritical. Just fiddle a bit with the dialogue if it doesn't ring right, but always give it a chance. Two – as a writer, or re-writer; where you have to analyze what isn't working, why moments are unsatisfying, what it needs, what is wrong with it. These are two totally different approaches, and they're not necessarily useful to each other.'

With Frank Morgan, Ralph has added another distinctive character to his long list; one who is decidedly unusual in the context of the smoke- and sweat-infused office of North West CID. Much more of a 'modern' copper, Morgan's adherence to protocol and the letter of the law mark him as a world apart from the likes of Gene Hunt. It was a new experience for *Life On Mars* viewers to see another policeman apart from Sam expressing views that could be described as politically correct.

'"Politically correct" is just a stupid way of

saying polite. I don't like rude people, especially if they're racist, but Gene Hunt makes a great TV character. He only works though through the prism of John Simm – who is us. They're a great team. I played a Gene Hunt-style character in the TV series *Lock Stock* … a fool called Miami Vice. I really enjoyed chewing the scenery, I must admit! Results are all that matter if you're a copper. Like Alan Shearer says: "How do you take a penalty, Alan?" "Stick it in the back of the net!" But seriously, we are policed by consent, and Brixton, Toxteth and Tottenham showed that the police had needed a smack in the mouth and a realignment of their approach.'

Despite the undeniable prejudices of the early seventies, is it an era of which he has fond memories?

'I certainly do. I wasn't allowed to grow my hair until 1972 so I became a johnny-come-lately hippy just as tear-drop collars were *de rigeur*. Luckily we had Bryan Ferry on hand to teach us sartorial elegance, David Bowie to open our minds and Status Quo to remind us that jeans were still okay. Labi Siffre's "It Must Be Love" was a big tune in our house, along with "Tired Of Being Alone" by Al Green and Lennon's "Imagine". *O Lucky Man* was the film, McDowell was the actor (along with John Hurt), Roxy Music were the band, *Lost in Space* and *Star Trek* were the TV shows.'

If he were to find himself in a 'coma world' like Sam Tyler what would it be?

'*Star Trek* probably, as the captain. You get to say "Warp Factor Two, Mr Sulu!" and "Thoughts, Spock?" and kiss the odd alien babe.'

Ah, but would that be something worth throwing yourself off a building to return to?

'Nothing is worth dying for. Saving my wife's life, for example, would make her totally miserable if I died.'

It's always a worry when talking to someone with such a prodigious background on screen that there's one obvious question that should have been asked, but wasn't. So, was there?

'Yes,' he replies without hesitation. '"Do you think that going bald has stopped you playing lead roles?" to which the answer would have been: "I certainly hope not, because I'm not about to do an Elton."'

Fair enough.

Living In The Past

Remembering The Seventies

The seventies was the decade that took us from the era of peace, love and the whiff of Patchouli through the closing years of war in Vietnam to the cold hard reality of strikes and the 'Winter of Discontent'. We thought we'd ask some of those we interviewed for this volume to cast their minds back and give us their memories of the era:

Ashley Pharoah

'Hmm... I was 13! Snogging Jackie Halfacre in a friend's garden. School camp on the Isle Of Wight, where every shop was playing 'Life on Mars?' Drinking pints of cider/Guinness mix for 15p; having a huge crush on Suzi Quatro; the lovely romance of a guttering candle in our front-room during the power strikes; the whole family snuggled together around the telly. Avon Ladies; discovering PG Wodehouse; the sound of leather on Brian Close at the County Ground in Taunton; seeing Ralph McTell at the Bristol Colston Hall...'

Chris Chibnall

'I have a memory of very hot and bleached out summers, that very sunny look, that's what my whole childhood looked like.'

Julie Rutterford

'I'll try to avoid the usual memories – platforms, glitter, the Three-Day Week and so on, and stick with one. In 1973, Jackie comic ran a competition where you had to write a love letter to David Cassidy – the prize was that you got to share a Curly Wurly with David or something like that. I was convinced I'd written the winning letter – unfortunately, in turquoise felt tip. I didn't win. I'm not bitter though. Bastards.'

Mark Greig

'Tank-tops. A two-tone denim suit and a bowl cut (stylish! Thanks, Mum…) Carpet with extravagant, psychedelic swirls of tangerine, brown and a unique shade of cowpat green. Clackers. The Banana Splits – "Size of a … DONKEY!" The Double Deckers (God, I wanted to live on that bus). Kung fu. Playing war. Till about '77, when life became something completely else…'

Matthew Graham

'I was stunned to see a set of curtains in the small Sam Tyler's bedroom that I had when I was a kid. Steam trains crossing both ways – red, green and brown (always brown back then!) Seeing those curtains billowing with a soundtrack made me want to cry.

Camberwick Green always filled me with a sense of nervous anticipation as to who would rise up from the musical box. It's a little like Don Giovanni, don't you think? Those stage productions that always have the Devil rise up on a dais and then drag the screaming Don back down into Hell. Yeah, okay, as a kid I probably wasn't calling Don Giovanni to mind but I still felt a sense of anxiety. And then when the character returned to stillness at the end and was lowered back into the box, I wondered if he was asleep. Dead? In suspended animation? Was it cosy in there? With books and a telly? Or was it dark and insanely claustrophobic. You can see why I was eventually taken off eating cheese by the time I was seven.

Hot car seats. I wish we'd mentioned hot car seats in the show. Baked up like griddles in the sun. You'd jump in the car after playing on the beach and receive third-degree burns to the backs of your legs. Summer of '76 – cook the kid. Calamine lotion. Slathering your sunburn in thick pink goo – it was like some arcane Crimean War field treatment.

What was that all about?'

Ralph Brown

'Losing my virginity and being in love (with the same person). Playing in a band – "Rough Justice" – we played covers of Beatles and Quo and some originals. Seeing Osibisa, Roxy Music, Focus, Alex Harvey, The Faces and Genesis live. Seeing ELO live! Taking LSD for the first time.

Watching The Long Goodbye, Sleeper, The Sting, The Last Detail and The Harder They Come at the Brighton Film Theatre. Watching The Exorcist in Brighton in a gang and having holy water sprinkled over us as we went in by Christians praying for our souls. The back two rows of the stalls were dedicated to the St John Ambulance and people were carrying their fainting girlfriends out of the cinema. Worst bit: the needle! Billie Jean King winning Wimbledon; "First Time Ever I Saw Your Face"; the Concert for Bangladesh (I bought that single!!). The Viet Cong winning the war – on May Day. I had a map of Vietnam on my bedroom wall with the American retreat in full colour…'

LOST AND FOUND:
THE FUGITIVE

'Would you just look at this?' Thompson said, face deep in the paper as they walked the short way between the newspaper office and the closest pub (there isn't a newspaper in the land that doesn't have at least one public house on emergency stand-by). 'Gene Hunt's wanted in connection with the murder of boxing promoter Terry Haslam! Gene Hunt! Wanted! Sounds like he finally snapped and popped someone.'

Never!' Adams replied. 'Not Mr Hunt, he's the best copper in the world and would never do such a thing.'

'Sod off,' Thompson replied, 'he's a raging nut-job who's always been one step short of a courtroom ever since we first clapped eyes on the psycho … oh.'

Thompson realised that Adams had stopped but he didn't know why until a few seconds after the fist burst through his newspaper and sent him sprawling.

'And you're a gobby little tosspot who has precisely three seconds to apologize before this raging nut-job shoves your head so far up your arse you'll be gargling with your bastard kidneys!'

'Sorry, Mr Hunt,' Thompson mumbled, clutching at his bleeding nose. 'Didn't see you there.'

'Obviously. Now, where's your car?'

Adams pointed at the tired looking Hillman Imp a few feet along the kerb. 'Just there.'

Hunt rolled his eyes. 'I said car, not roller skate: what's the bloody thing run on, mice?'

'Best we could afford. Sorry.' Adams looked awkward. 'I take it you want a lift?'

'I wasn't making party conversation, was I? Come on!'

They marched over to the car, Thompson being shoved rudely in the back as Hunt took the passenger seat. Adams climbed in and turned the ignition. Then he did it again. The third time actually made the engine rumble and he slowly pulled the car out onto the road.

'Where are we going, then?' he asked.

'Turn left at the end. I'll direct you as we go.'

'I'm bleeding on the seats back here,' Thompson moaned.

'Do it quietly,' Hunt growled.

'What's it all about, then?' Adams asked. 'On the run and all that.'

'I'm being framed,' Hunt replied.

'You and Dr Richard Kimble,' Thompson muttered from the back. 'Did a one-armed man do it?'

Hunt leaned over the seat to stare at Thompson. 'I might just forget the fact that I am a man of honour and integrity in a minute and give plod a real corpse to pin on me.'

'Sorry.'

'You bloody will be. Turn right.'

'Eh? Oh…' Adams swung the wheel, secretly praying the car wouldn't fall apart, and followed Hunt's directions.

'Keep going to the end and then turn right again. Hattershall's gym is just along on the left.'

'Hattershall's gym?'

'Yeah, I'm off to do a bit of investigating.'

'Should we alert the ambulance service?' Thompson asked.

They drove the rest of the way in silence, except for Thompson's occasional moans as he massaged his newly

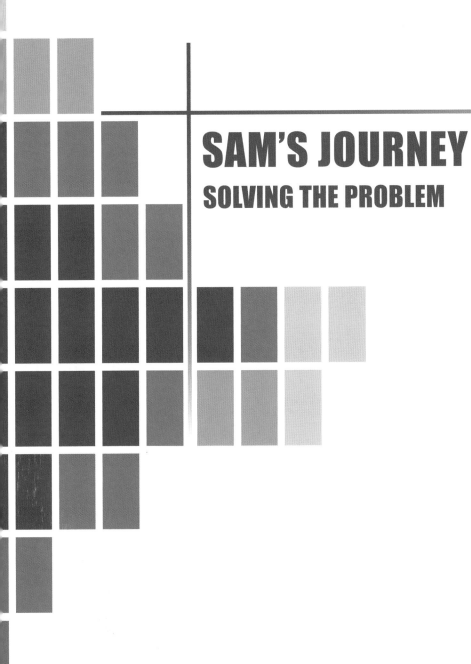

SAM'S JOURNEY
SOLVING THE PROBLEM

'My name is Sam Tyler. I had an
accident, and I woke up in 1973. Am
I mad, in a coma, or back in time?
Whatever's happened, it's like I've
landed on a different planet.
Now maybe if I can work out the
reason, I can get home...'

Sam's voiceover, as heard over the title
sequence

EPISODE ONE

We're back in 1973 and things are surreal from
the off inside poor Sam Tyler's head as he is
taunted by eerie sounds from the future –
whistling and threats.

Next moment, Gene's waking him up and
they're on their way to a crime scene. A man
has been found on the upper deck of a bus with
his head caved in. Linking a poker chip found
near the body with the Wildcard Casino that lies
on the bus route the victim was travelling, Sam
and Gene give the gaming club a visit. Casino
owner Tony Crane is known to Sam from the
future; one of the last cases he tackled before
his accident was assembling evidence against
Crane – by that time a highly successful, and
criminal, gaming boss. The question is, can
Sam stop him before he starts? Things become
even more complicated when Sam realises that
Crane is standing by his hospital bed in the
future and will kill his comatose body if he gets
the chance...

■ **FUTURE BLEED:** 'How's he doing?' Sam
hears the doctor enquire at the start of the
episode, before a ghostly whistling of 'Bring Me
Sunshine' turns the vision into a nightmare.
Woken up by Gene kicking his door down, Sam's
back in 1973, until he hears the whistling again
at the violent crime scene. A billboard poster of
Morecambe and Wise asks us to 'Keep Britain
Tidy' as Sam sees the spectral shape of his
attacker on the transformed shell of a television

set. Do Eric and Ernie know that their signature
tune is being used to intimidate?

Crane is haunting Sam from the future and the
visions persist – through the fish tank in Crane's
casino office; in bed as the realisation hits Sam
that Crane has killed his wife (one of Sam's key
witnesses in the case); over the telephone in the
canteen; in the corridor outside the CID office as
his 1973 self is sent blind by Crane toying with
him in the present. Finally, on his knees as Crane
speeds towards him, Sam is split between past
and present as he nears death in both eras.

■ **PROMOTIONS:** Ray is bumped back up to
DS and is told by Gene to 'make it stand for
"Detective Sergeant" rather than "dog shit"
this time.' Annie is promoted from uniform to
CID, much to the wolf-whistled cynicism of the
department.

DOUBLE MEANINGS: A man awaiting sectioning echoes Sam's own loose grip on this 'reality'. 'No one believes me but it's true,' he shouts, as the officers try and restrain him. 'I see things … the world isn't what they think. How do you think that makes me feel?'

DO YOU WANT TO KNOW WHERE I REALLY COME FROM? Sam seems hell-bent on getting himself committed as he nearly blurts out his story to the whole of CID. Later, he does tell Tony Crane about his car crash and his belief that Crane's older self is trying to kill him in the future. Crane subsequently repeats Sam's accusations as proof that Sam's insane and the case against him is going to crumble because of it. Sam turns the tables on him by citing it as sufficient proof that *Crane* is delusional enough to be sectioned.

SAM/ANNIE: Their relationship grows stronger and Annie is learning from Sam's policing skills. She's cordoning off crime scenes and hunting for clues with her eyebrow tweezers (although she claims this last was learned from McGill in *Man in a Suitcase*, a TV series from the late sixties). Despite being disturbed by Sam's persistent talk of the future she stands by him and supports him even in his excesses. 'You can't convict him from a padded cell,' she warns, desperate to keep him together. They nearly kiss before Sam finds himself unable to breathe from Crane interfering with his oxygen in the future…

ANNIE MOMENT: Having been promoted to CID she gets her own back on Ray slapping her arse by giving him a touch of his own medicine, commenting that his is 'like suet in a bag'.

MAKING HISTORY: Sam invents 'the Stinger', a spiked chain used to halt speeding cars.

GENE MOMENT: 'Black suits you, Meadows. Do you want an eye in the same colour?' Desperate to gather leads, Gene drags a known

mugger from the funeral of his father and threatens to 'kick the crap' out of the ashes unless he gives him some information.

■ **HYDE CALLING:** At the end of the first episode Sam's telephone rings and he has his first conversation with his mysterious 'boss' in Hyde.

'Sam, I know you can't talk to me now,' says the man on the line. 'I can hear you, I can always hear you,' Sam mutters, thinking this is just one of the usual rips in his reality. 'I know you can hear me, Sam,' the voice replies, much to Sam's surprise, 'but I need you to listen.' 'What…? Wait… How can we be talking?' Sam can't believe he's actually talking to someone. 'I need you to get me out of here.' 'And we will,' says the voice. 'I understand your frustration, Sam, but the job's almost done, don't blow it now.' 'Job?' asks Sam, more confused than ever. 'Remember,' says the voice, 'if they find out why you're really there, you'll never make it back. Once we've dealt with it all you can come home, Sam.' Then the man hangs up.

EPISODE TWO

Sam, Chris and Ray are instructed to have safe-cracker Richard Hands (aka Dickie Fingers) released from prison to assist with their investigation into a spate of robberies. On the way from the prison they are driven off the road by a gang of armed men who kidnap Dickie. This doesn't impress Gene: 'I've seen cesspits with more brains,' he comments before informing the team that Superintendent Harry Woolf is to be part of the investigation. Woolf is convinced that not only is his long-standing nemesis, Arnold Malone, responsible for Fingers' abduction, but that he is the man behind most of the big hauls in the Manchester area. It's to be Woolf's last case and if he can retire knowing that he's finally put Malone behind bars, he'll be a happy man.

By putting the word out amongst their informants the best they can get is a single name: Harcourt. An extra pair of hands is brought in from C Division to help go through the archives: Glen Fletcher, a rare black face in the context of CID. The young Fletcher takes a pragmatic

attitude to the casual racism endemic in the seventies. 'Don't worry,' he tells the team, eager to get onside, 'if there's a power cut I'll roll my eyes and you can follow me to the exit.' Sam, who will be Fletcher's protégé in years to come, is appalled to hear his future mentor resigned to making jokes at his own expense, and urges him to speak out against bigotry rather than play along. Fletcher is dubious that there is much of a future for a black policeman, especially one who makes waves, but Sam, knowing what Fletcher will go on to achieve, tells him to have more belief in himself.

When a wages van is knocked off it becomes clear that Dickie Fingers was the man who cracked the safe. Woolf insists that Malone and Fingers were in cahoots from the start, but Sam is less convinced: he remembers how scared Fingers was when he was dragged off by the gunmen. Threatened by Gene, Malone offers proof that it wasn't him who snatched Fingers by telling them where the next robbery will take place: the main post office in Raxton Street. With less than an hour to go, Gene gets everyone moving and under cover, determined to catch the crooks in the act. Meanwhile, on his way to the post office, Sam finds Woolf keeled over with a hip flask. It's not what he thinks, however, as Woolf reveals that he's on medication for terminal cancer, with less than a year to live. Gene doesn't know, and Woolf wants it to stay that way.

The post office robbery foiled and Fingers back behind bars, Fingers agrees to give Sam the name of the person behind the robberies, provided Sam can promise him protection. That name is Harry Woolf. Sam is sceptical, but he arranges to keep Fingers in custody for another twenty-four hours so that he can investigate further. He tells Hunt, who loses his rag and pops down to the cells to beat Fingers up a bit. Gene also tells Woolf, who surprises him by insisting that Sam investigates the allegation. He claims to take his reputation seriously and is determined to play everything by the book.

Overnight, a fight breaks out and Fingers escapes. When he turns up dead, it comes to

light that Fletcher, who was on cell duty that night, let him walk – under Woolf's orders. Woolf claims he wanted Fingers out of custody so that he could follow him and catch him and Malone together; except that Fingers got away, leaving him, Woolf, looking guilty.

Gene and Sam go and see Malone, hoping to intimidate him into confessing and clear Woolf's name. Malone won't play. He claims to have evidence on Woolf and, now that the man has crossed the line by killing Fingers, they're welcome to it.

Gene finally begins to see that his mentor is bent and all he can do now is make sure that the division cleans up its own mess by taking Woolf down. Arranging for Fletcher to get Woolf out of the way for a couple of hours so that they can search his office, Sam and Gene find a building society book in the name of 'Harcourt' Woolf: matching the deposits up with the robbery dates, they know they have their man. Then they find a stash of hidden money – which is when Woolf returns.

Trying to appeal to Gene's mercy, he pleads

his illness and begs to be given the chance to run with the money. Gene won't have it. It's time to make a stand and Woolf must account for what he's done. Guns are drawn, threats are given. Glen Fletcher appears, his face still swollen with the bruises of Woolf's violence. In the end Woolf smiles as he asks: 'Which of us is going to have the balls to shoot first?' With no pause at all, Gene shoots him in the leg, and it's all over.

■ **FUTURE BLEED:** While Gene talks to an informant, Sam sees an advertising board for the *Manchester Evening News* reading: 'Sam Tyler: we are sorry for your loss.' Looking at the paper he sees a report that Glen Fletcher, Manchester's first black Deputy Chief Constable, has died of a heart attack. Through the ever-present sound of his life support machine Sam remembers the time when Fletcher made him a DCI. He is shocked back to present by the sight of two identical twins on a tandem. They want to know the winner at Aintree…

Later, when Fletcher – still only a DC in 1973

– walks into the office, Sam sees him as the old man he will become.

■ KEY MOMENT: Sam and Gene, having found the money and building society book in Woolf's office, are warned of his arrival by the bell of the CID lift. They move out into the corridor to intercept him. He tries to bluff his way out of the situation but it's too late for that; Gene no longer believes him. 'Et tu, Gene,' Woolf says, referencing Shakespeare's *Julius Caesar*. 'You believe all these things you hear about me?' 'Talk me out of it, tell me it's all untrue,' is Gene's measured reply. Woolf thinks about it but, with a sigh, concedes it's gone too far for that. 'I can't… I made you too good.'

■ GENE MOMENT: Stood outside Malone's warehouse Gene gives Sam a gun and asks him to wave it about a bit once they get inside. 'Have you never heard of "softly softly"?' Sam protests. 'Yes,' replies Gene. 'But I prefer *Z Cars*.'

Later, Sam wonders aloud how Gene's wife can possibly put up with him. 'Must be my legendary prowess as a lover,' is Gene's response.

■ RAY MOMENT: As DC Glen Fletcher is introduced, Ray makes his feelings only too clear: 'First women, now a coloured. What's going to be next? Dwarves?'

■ ANNIE MOMENT: Annie complains that she hasn't received any firearms training. 'You see, this is why birds and CID don't mix,' Gene sighs. 'You give a bloke a gun and it's a dream come true. You give a girl one and she moans it doesn't go with her dress. Start behaving like a detective and show some balls!' 'Thanks for being so supportive, Sir,' she replies. 'Let's hope you don't end up in my firing line.'

Later, when one of the armed robbers has his shotgun pointed at her face, she shouts: 'Put that any closer and I'll smack you in the mouth!' 'Not that ballsy, you tart!' mutters Gene from where he, Sam and Woolf are observing.

■ PHYLLIS MOMENT: Annie is not alone in doing her bit for ballsy women. When Phyllis is also threatened by a shotgun she is cavalier enough to comment: 'Look at yourself. Women's undies on your head, pointing a gun at a woman: how small must your John Thomas be?'

■ SAM/GENE: Sam and Gene grow ever closer during this episode – despite a slight hitch in their friendship as Gene shuts Sam in the boot of the Cortina for investigating Woolf. By the end they are sat in the Railway Arms,

prospect of a woman PM as unlikely. 'If Margaret Thatcher ever becomes Prime Minister,' he replies, putting his hip flask away in his pocket, 'I'll have been doing something a lot stronger than whisky.'

'You read much Freud, DI Tyler?' Woolf asks Sam during the final standoff. 'I'm more of a Dan Brown man,' Sam replies.

■ HYDE CALLING: Glen Fletcher remembers Sam from Hyde: 'I was in Hyde for a bit … weren't

talking first about Sam's plans for holding staff appraisals before, inevitably, conversation turns back to the fate of Harry Woolf. Sam wonders if Woolf will be left to die penniless and alone, something Gene insists he will not allow. 'Do you want my appraisal of you?' Sam offers with a smile. 'No,' Gene replies. There is a pause before Sam smiles again and raises his glass. 'It's your round then.' Gene nods and stands up, thinks for a moment, then says, genuinely: 'Thank you.'

■ I HAVE SEEN THE FUTURE: Sam continues to show altogether too much knowledge for his own good, predicting to Woolf that Margaret Thatcher (then Education Secretary) will be Prime Minister. The old copper dismisses the

there a bit of bother?' Luckily for Sam, they are interrupted before he is forced to give any more information. But at the end of the episode, Sam phones the Hyde number. 'Hello?' the same voice as before answers. 'Who is this?' Sam asks. 'Sam? Sam, is that you?' the voice replies. 'You've been making calls to my phone,' Sam accuses, trying to extract some detail – any detail – from the caller. 'Don't call here again, Sam,' the voice warns. This is a breach of protocol. 'You know the rules,' the voice insists. 'What rules?' protests Sam. 'I call you,' the voice replies. 'Who are you?' Sam hisses, desperate now. But the voice on the other end of the line hangs up.

EPISODE THREE

A call is received at headquarters warning of a dynamite bomb placed outside a school. The bomb is being attributed to the IRA but Sam is suspicious as they have never used dynamite. The IRA use homemade explosives: weed killer and sugar. Convinced the bomb is a hoax, Sam is cajoled to go and check it out by Ray. They argue and Sam challenges Ray to go over and investigate. Unless he's lost his bottle, of course. The bomb goes off and Ray is seriously hurt.

Sam is determined to prove it's not the IRA: he studied terrorist methods as part of his training and knows that he's right. He and Gene investigate a building site from which fifty pounds of dynamite is missing. Site foreman Frank Miller shows them around. It would only take a couple of pounds of dynamite to blow up a car, so they have to accept that there is still a dangerous quantity left on the street.

Sam begs Gene to tread carefully as he knows that if they antagonise the Irish workers they'll have the whole Irish community against them and then they'll get nowhere. Searching the lockers, they find a denim jacket belonging to a man called Patrick O'Brien, its pockets containing pamphlets for the rights of Irish immigrants, details of rallies and meetings. There is also a list of street names. They interrogate O'Brien but he gives them nothing. Gene is beating him up when another call comes in. A car bomb again, this time outside a pub. Fifteen minutes to detonation.

The bomb squad is late, delayed by a hoax call. Sam has defused a bomb once before and hopes he can remember which wire to cut as he pushes himself under the chassis with a pair of pliers. Red or yellow? He thinks it's red but it's so hard to be sure… The bomb is about to go off when the bomb squad arrive in the nick of time and one of them cuts the red wire.

They notice that the car was parked on one of the streets on O'Brien's list, although

he claims that they are just streets where the building contractor has completed jobs. Things are looking increasingly bad for O'Brien when he goes missing and Phyllis receives warning of a large bomb due to go off in four hours. But Sam is even more sceptical now … the IRA would never give that much warning.

Following a hunch, Sam returns to the building site, where he finds a bank statement showing how deep in debt Frank Miller is. He and Annie check off the list of names found in O'Brien's jacket against the old jobs in Miller's files. The one omission is Kennel Road, for which they find building plans of underground tunnels that would allow access to a bank's vaults. Sam suspects that Miller is sending them on a wild goose chase by planting the list on O'Brien. A phone call comes in telling the police that the bomb is on Clay Street, but Sam is convinced that it's a con: that the bomb will actually be on Kennel Road and the whole thing has not been political at all, but a smokescreen to hide Miller's planned bank raid.

The team access the tunnels and catch Miller in the act.

■ **GENE'S GUIDE TO INTERROGATION:** When Patrick O'Brien is pulled out of his Union meeting, he tells Hunt: 'You're an even bigger bastard than I remember.' Gene shrugs. 'Maybe your memory's playing tricks on you.' Then he punches him hard in the gut. 'No. You're right. I am a bigger bastard.'

■ **SAM/ANNIE:** Despite sharing the concerns of the rest of CID that Sam's mistake put Ray in hospital, Annie allows him to convince her that he's right in suspecting Miller. In the end she helps him search the foreman's office where they gather the evidence to convict him. At the end of the episode Sam tells her: 'Listen. I forgot to say thanks. I owe you one.' 'For what?' she replies. 'For helping me,' says Sam. Annie brushes it off, although she can tell Sam is genuinely touched by her support. 'A Kit Kat will do nicely,' she tells him. 'Tell you what,' he smiles, about to blow it, if only he knew. 'Seeing as it's you, I'll make it a chunky one.' 'Chunky?' she scoffs, disappointed in him – being years away from that particular confection, she assumes he's referring to something entirely different.

■ **ANNIE MOMENT:** When Miller has a gun to Ray's head, it is Annie who starts to talk him down by making him think about how his daughter would feel. She is proving herself a strong member of the team already.

■ **FUTURE BLEED:** At the opening of the episode Sam's radio starts to crackle and lose its station, while the Open University is playing on his television and discussion of geometry morphs into concern over Sam's mental condition after being in a coma so long. Two doctors are talking by his hospital bed, one seemingly convinced that Sam's brain is operating just as it should, the other not sure. 'The mind's a fragile thing,' pipes up one voice from his radio. 'Who's to say what's been damaged?'

AN LÁRIONAD EIREANNACH
IRISH COMMUNITY CENTRE

'There's no evidence to suggest a decline,' the Open University lecturer argues. 'What are you basing your judgement on, guesswork?' 'No, Dr Matthews,' the radio replies. 'It's called instinct.' This starts a running theme throughout the episode regarding Sam's instincts and judgement. Does he cut the red or yellow wire? Does he trust his gut? The car radio later asks: 'What do you think Sam? What do we do?' but, as ever, Sam is unable to answer.

In the end the phone rings at the Railway Arms and, picking it up, Sam is reassured to hear the doctor say, 'Despite our fears, you have demonstrated evidence of healthy brain activity. But … you must continue to believe and trust in yourself, Sam, like we believe and trust in you.' Although Sam doesn't know it at the time (and nor do we), the doctor's voice is of course that of Frank Morgan.

■ **BIN WATCH:** Score one to Gene at 51' 32. That's how a real man parks.

■ **A TOUCH OF THE IRISH:** The other running theme of the exploitation of Irish immigrants

culminates in a heartfelt speech from the wrongly accused O'Brien: 'I'll never get a chance to run me own business,' he shouts at Gene, highlighting the difference between him and Miller, 'send my kids to the best school, drive a fancy motor: do you know why? All our kind are good for is shovelling shit and making bombs, is that right?' Gene doesn't answer. 'You know what, big lad,' O'Brien continues, 'I'm sick of shovelling shit.'

■ **GENE MOMENT:** When Ray returns, battered and bruised from the bomb blast but determined to help catch the bastard who blew him up, Sam, with his twenty-first century knowledge of post-traumatic stress, tries to convince Gene that Ray shouldn't be there as he's suffering from PTSD. 'The man's a hero,' Gene exclaims, 'and you're accusing him of having the clap.'

■ **SAM MOMENT:** At the end of the episode when he walks into the Railway Arms he gets a round of applause, just as Ray did when he came out of hospital.

■ **I HAVE SEEN THE FUTURE:** Annie comments that 'maybe we would be better off if a woman did run the country, she couldn't make a worse job than the fellers have done of it.' Sam, always eager to drop hints about the future, replies: 'I've a feeling you'll regret saying that one day.'

■ **DOUBLE MEANINGS:** 'Let me know when you're back living in the real world, Tyler,' says Gene at one point. 'If only,' Sam replies.

Later, while on the hunt for O'Brien, Sam goes into a church and sits in the confessional. 'I'm not really what you would call a religious man, Father,' he says, 'I don't go to church, don't pray, can't stand Cliff Richard… This isn't even a confession, it's just that right now I'm lost and there's nobody I can talk to. I shouldn't even be here.'

■ **SAM/GENE:** Sam doesn't quite see eye to eye with Gene's willingness to leap on the Irish connection. 'Phyllis,' Gene bellows into the police radio, 'it might be a good idea to go through all the "O"s in the phone book.' 'Oh!' Sam shouts sarcastically, 'Tell you what, while we're at it why don't we pull in that well-known terrorist suspect Dana? How about Val Doonican?'

Their relationship is stretched dangerously thin in this episode as Sam's conviction nearly costs the life of one of the department. In the end, though, Sam is able to prove his worth.

■ **TEST CARD GIRL:** Returns for the first time in this series. 'Red lorry yellow lorry, red wire yellow wire…' she chants, holding out two matches, one red, one yellow, like the wires in the bomb Sam couldn't defuse. 'Pick one: you pick the right one and it proves you were right. It's okay, Sam, I know you'll pick the right one. Go with your instinct.' He picks the red. 'Bang. You're dead, Sam,' she says. 'Oh dear. You and how many others?'

EPISODE FOUR

On a section of wasteland the body of a woman in her twenties has been found. Sam notices a distinctive smell on her hair but is at a loss to place it. In her hands she is holding a crushed red geranium, which harks back to a high-profile investigation from five years ago; a serial killer known as 'Manc the Knife'. A suspect, Terence Finn, was convicted and died in prison. Did they get the wrong man, or is this a copycat killing?

On his way home Sam sees a woman thrown out of a car and leaps to her rescue. She seems unharmed but he takes her for a drink to find out what happened. The woman, Denise Williams, has the same distinctive perfume he recognised on the murder victim's hair. It is a perfume Sam associates with his Auntie Heather as she – as well as Denise – worked as a 'Beauvoir Lady', selling cosmetic products door-to-door. Denise insists that the driver who threw her from the car was a stranger and vanishes while Sam is ordering them another drink.

Meanwhile a husband who reported his wife missing identifies the body: her name is Sandra Trotman and she too is a Beauvoir Lady. Sam and Annie pick up Denise for questioning, and once they tell her the identity of the murdered woman she begins to talk. She worked with Sandra at 'swinging parties' organised by car salesman Roger Twilling. Sam and Gene investigate the car showroom and Sam recognises the car from which Denise was thrown. Then Sam finds out that Twilling was friends with the original pathologist on the murder case: he guesses that was how Twilling heard about the red geranium MO and has used it to throw the police off the scent. Gradually the net begins to close…

Sam and Annie go undercover as a young couple new to the area, Tony and Cherie Blair. They get chatting to Twilling and his wife invites them to a party that same evening: nothing fancy, just 'some nicely chilled Blue Nun and a few vol-au-vents.' At the party, evidently having passed muster with the Twillings, they find themselves invited to a swingers' evening, and are just getting into the thick of it – car keys are on the table and the swapping is about to begin – when Gene turns up. In a panic Sam introduces Gene as his friend Gordon Brown and his wife … Suki. Suki, it transpires, is a prostitute that Gene let off for lewd behaviour a week ago. 'Well,' he says, 'you didn't think I'd bring me own wife, did you?'

Twilling accepts Sam's story and 'Gordon Brown' duly joins the party. Everyone pairs off, Annie with Twilling, Sam with Twilling's wife and Gene with the unnerving Mrs Luckhurst. Sam manages to ignore the sound of Gene's discomfort as Mrs Luckhurst has her wicked way but when he hears Annie shouting he breaks cover, only to find her stood over Twilling with a whip in her hand – apparently he had been beginning to talk.

Twilling's lawyer, however, insists on 'no comment' throughout questioning and it is only thanks to Annie's foresight in placing a hidden microphone in his car that the case doesn't fall apart. Hearing the sound of Denise begging for her life, they rush to Twilling's house only to find Denise is in the car with Carol, Twilling's wife. *She* killed Sandra after her husband had an affair with her and she got jealous. Pursuing the vengeful Carol, they are just in time to stop her killing Denise.

■ **HISTORICAL ROOTS (1):** The Beauvoir Ladies were inspired by the famous Avon Products, founded in America in 1886 by door-to-door salesman David H. McConnell, who gave away free perfume to the women he did business with, hoping to encourage them to buy his books. He soon realised that the perfume was much more popular than the books and changed direction. The female sales staff of Avon Products were known as 'Avon Ladies' and greeted customers

desperate to hear the voices that seep through it from the future. He spends most of the episode trying to fix it.

He hears his aunt again briefly on the police radio but the station is lost in seconds. Later, while jogging, he answers a ringing phone box and hears her voice. 'Auntie Heather?' he asks, but she puts the phone down, telling him he has the wrong number. He then meets her in the flesh as one of the many Beauvoir Ladies

with the now legendary slogan, 'Avon calling!' which was created as part of an international sales campaign in 1954.

■ **HISTORICAL ROOTS (2):** Blue Nun is one of the most famous (and derided) wine labels in the UK. Hugely popular in the seventies, its unchallenging Liebfraumilch composition made it the choice of a middle class eager to avoid the Gothic lettered complexity of other German wines. Allegedly the favourite drink of fictional DJ Alan Partridge it was re-branded in the noughties with a changed blend of grapes to make it more palatable, leading to something of a revival.

■ **FUTURE BLEED:** At the start of the episode Sam dreams of his Auntie Heather looking after him while he was ill. Sam's telly appears to be broken and he finds that, more than ever, he's

they bring in for questioning, but he realises that he can't speak to her; she'll never believe who he is. At the end of the episode, however, he finally fixes his TV and sees her looking down on his hospital bed in the future, reassuring him that she'll always be there for him.

■ **POLICE SCHEDULING:** 'Find out who the dead woman was, find out who killed her. Do it now!' Gene Hunt shouts to the rest of CID, before glancing at his watch. 'Hold up, hold up,' he continues, not missing a beat, 'do it tomorrow morning, first thing. Beer o'clock, gentlemen!'

■ **SAM/ANNIE:** Worried for her safety with a killer on on the loose, Sam tries to walk Annie home, but she won't let him. 'Are you walking Chris and Ray home?' she asks, a little indignantly. 'I don't need your help, I can walk myself home, Sir.' They work together throughout the case, posing as husband and wife, and there are many moments when the show of closeness they put on for the suspects threatens to become real. At the end he tries to walk her home again but she's meeting up with friends, and, awkwardly, they go their separate ways.

■ **I HAVE SEEN THE FUTURE:** Sam makes great use of rudimentary recording equipment – all valves and wires – as he tries to instruct CID on the merits of hidden surveillance. They seem to understand only too well as the first use the machinery is put to is eavesdropping on Annie in the loo.

■ **CHRIS MOMENT:** Chris still hasn't quite found the right way to behave at a crime scene. 'Any sign of sexual assault?' Gene asks him when the body is first found. 'Hard to tell, Guv,' he replies before hoisting up the victim's skirt and exposing her to officers and onlookers alike. 'She's still got her knickers on.'

■ **THE CID GUIDE TO DATING:** A running theme through the episode is Chris's attempts to have a successful night out with a girl he met at an ice rink (by skating over her finger). 'Take my advice,' Ray offers, 'get a pint of Pernod and Black down her, do what you like to her after that.' 'What are you hoping for, upstairs inside?' Gene asks. 'It's got to be inside downstairs, Guv!' Ray suggests, in shock at Hunt's lack of ambition on Chris's behalf. 'What? On a first date?' Gene replies. 'She's not a prozzy … is she?' Chris assures him she isn't. 'First date: upstairs inside,' Gene repeats, sure of his stuff.

Later Chris is forced to admit to them all that he threw up his own pint of Pernod and Black 'over her face … her mouth…' It wasn't a good date. He does get a second chance though and, with a little advice from Sam, manages to have a good time.

EPISODE FIVE

'This is a box, a magical box, playing a magical tune. But inside this box is a surprise. Do you know who's inside it today? It's Sam Tyler. Hello Sam, how are you today? Oh dear, not very happy… Is it Gene Hunt? Is he kicking in a nonce?'

Sam is feverish, dreaming of a Camberwick Green in which both he and Gene appear as stop-frame animated characters. His phone rings – it's Chris, asking if he's still off sick. He sees Chris on the television, Ray stood behind him: how can he be watching them as they talk to him over the phone? Then his radio speaks to him, telling him that he has been given an overdose of medication which has put him in extreme clinical danger. *Freaky, baby!*

After a weird journey where the streets blur around him, Sam arrives at CID to see a man

trying to hang himself. The man is Simon Lamb, a PE teacher, and he is desperate because his wife and daughter have been kidnapped to bargain the release of Graham Bathurst, a young man convicted of the murder of fourteen-year-old schoolgirl Charley Witham.

Sam, his metabolism still wired, must sort through the details of this old case and try and get to the bottom of it. Interviewing the members of CID to get an understanding of what happened he discovers that Charley Witham was asphyxiated, an oily rag shoved in her mouth. Graham was her boyfriend and the number one suspect. Determined to have the case solved – as much for Charley's parents' sake as his own – Gene pulled no punches when interrogating Bathurst, ultimately making it clear to him that if he signed a confession he would get off with a shorter sentence. After constant intimidation, Bathurst signed. But was Gene too forceful? Did he misread the evidence? Annie begins to suspect so and, after re-reading a letter from Charley's parents accusing the police of incompetence she begins to wonder if Don Witham, Charley's father, may be behind the Lamb family's abduction.

As the doctors in the future give Sam a counter-dose to try and stabilise him he becomes unconscious and observes the rest of the events on a TV. He sees Annie visit Charley's parents and watches helplessly as she herself is endangered, discovering Lamb's wife and daughter in the garden shed just before Don Witham catches her.

Back at CID they are coming to the same conclusion. Lamb was sent photographs of his family where he had been removed from the picture. The photographs were taken at his daughter's recent birthday party by a man that both he and his wife had assumed the other to have hired. They are looking for a photographer with the skill to doctor images. Don Witham works for the newspaper as a photographer and prepares the Spot The Ball competition. They arrive at Witham's house in time to save Annie, Sam cheering them on from the strange, dark room in his subconscious.

Sam is feeling himself once more as he and Gene watch Simon Lamb happily reunited with his family. Gene is reassured that it appears he wasn't wrong in suspecting Bathurst. He tells Sam of the Tung oil they found on the rag in Charley's mouth and how they linked that to Bathurst's hobby of repairing motorbikes.

Something in Sam's head clicks. Tung oil isn't used on engines, it's for polishing wood;

and Lamb stated that on the night Charley was murdered he had been in the gym, polishing the equipment. Sam and Gene look at Lamb and see him glance briefly at a young girl going past. It's a small gesture but enough. Maybe Bathurst was wrongly imprisoned after all.

Together, they head towards Lamb…

■ **FUTURE BLEED:** The effects of Sam's unintentional drug overdose make this episode more surreal than most. The radio warns him what has happened and, later, a sheet in his typewriter reads: 'We're trying to block the effects, Sam.' The effect of the drug put into his system knocks him unconscious and he experiences most of the latter part of the episode in a small room, watching events unfold on a TV screen.

■ **CHRIS MOMENT:** Proving less than adept at talking down a potential suicide he comes out with the gem: 'I always say there's a time to take off the noose and put on the kettle.' Needless to say, it doesn't work.

■ **SAM/GENE:** Wired from the drugs in his system and fresh from his hallucination of Gene as an animated clay thug, Sam storms into CID and grabs his boss by the lapels. 'As for you,' he shouts, 'get this straight. I can just about handle you driving like a pissed up crack-head and treating women like bean bags, but I'm going to say this once and once only, Gene – stay out of Camberwick Green!'

■ **RAY MOMENT:** 'I haven't been to the pub in thirty-six hours!' Ray shouts. 'Shit,' Sam replies, aware of how serious the situation is.

■ **ANNIE MOMENT:** Annie again proves her worth to CID both by piecing together the trail leading to Don Witham and by her willingness to stand up to Gene. 'Supposing,' she says to him, 'we made mistakes. Back in '72. And

supposing those mistakes have come back to haunt us.' This doesn't go down well with Gene, but in the end he is forced to acknowledge she was right.

■ **SAM/ANNIE:** When Sam is stuck as an observer he watches Annie notice an advert for a Roxy Music gig and glance at his leather jacket. When he is back on his feet he wastes little time in inviting her out on a date. 'I'm feeling … I'm feeling good,' he says, head finally free of the drugs. 'Let's go out somewhere. One night this week.' 'What have you got in mind?' she asks. To this Sam just *knows* he's onto a winner. 'Roxy Music at the Free Trade Hall.' 'I'll think about it,' she replies with a grin.

Episode Six

Dipak Gandhi, a Ugandan Asian, is found on the floor of the record shop he co-owns with his brother Ravi, a gunshot wound in his chest and several wraps of heroin in his pocket. Annie finds a pulse and Dipak is rushed to hospital, while a young woman is found in the back room who claims she was there as a customer but hid when she heard the shot.

Gene reckons that Dipak was shot as part of a turf war amongst dealers, so he and Sam go to see Rocket, a known dealer, who says that he'd 'rather have rabid ferrets eat his testicles than help the filth.' Gene throws him through a wall to see if he can change his mind, whereupon Rocket confirms that Gandhi was dealing heroin out of his shop.

Back at the shop Sam finds the young woman, Layla, who was hiding there when they found the victim. Clearly more than a customer, she admits that she used to help them with their accounts. Sam is aware of a powerful attraction between them, but he doesn't know why – only that she reminds him of someone. She shows him where the letters 'NF' (National Front) have been sprayed on the wall of the shop and Sam begins to wonder if there is more of a racial angle to all this. 'I think we need to consider whether this attempted murder was a hate crime,' he says, to which Gene replies in typical pithy fashion, 'As opposed to one of those I-really-like-you sort of murders?'

Toolbox Terry, a local hard man, claims to want to put a stop to the spread of imported heroin. Sam is outraged when Gene allows Toolbox and his accomplice Big Bird (a large woman) to interrogate Rocket – with the aid of a bag of ferrets. Rocket later implicates Ravi Gandhi in the attack on Dipak, saying the brothers argued about the drugs money. He also lets slip that Layla is Dipak's girlfriend.

Sam is furious because she lied to him and he believed her. But being the soft touch he is, he takes her to visit the still unconscious Dipak and then to his flat after they discover hers has been torched by racist thugs. Is the reason Sam feels a connection with Layla to do with the fact that both of them are in mixed race relationships – she with Dipak and he with Maya in the future? Or maybe there's more to it. 'This girlfriend of yours … what was she like?' asks Layla. 'Oh,' says Sam, 'smart and stubborn and funny … a bit like you.'

From then on issues of trust and betrayal dominate this episode as suspicion falls first on Ravi and then on Layla – especially when Dipak is stabbed to death in his hospital bed and she was seen at his bedside – and then on Ravi again, as the crates in which he imports the belongings of his fellow Ugandan Asians are revealed to contain hidden heroin after all. Then Sam finds out that Layla is Maya's mother – no wonder he felt drawn to her – and that Dipak is Maya's father. Pregnant with an illegitimate baby whose father has just been murdered, Layla is determined to have an abortion, but Sam manages to dissuade her by telling her what a wonderful daughter she'll have. ('She'll have

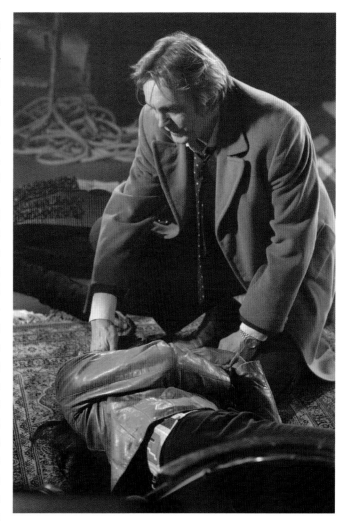

great taste in men,' he adds.) Layla thinks he's crazy, of course – but at the same time there's something truly compelling in his sincerity and conviction.

Sam also works out that Toolbox, Big Bird and Rocket are smuggling the heroin and that they set up the Gandhis to take the rap – but it may be too late, as Toolbox and Big Bird hold Sam, Gene, Annie and Ravi at gunpoint and coolly set about making it look like Ravi shot the coppers in a stand-off. As Big Bird levels her gun at Sam a shot rings out – but it's from Chris, who, much to his own astonishment, comes to their rescue at the eleventh hour, taking down Big Bird and saving the day for them all.

■ **SAM/GENE:** Having found the bound and beaten Ravi Gandhi at an abandoned cinema, Sam wants to get him out before Toolbox kills him. Gene, believing that the best way to solve the drug problem is to let the crooks police one another, no questions asked, is happy to turn a blind eye. Sam is disgusted. 'If you do this,' he shouts, 'there's no turning back, you know that, don't you? When you look in the mirror there'll be a different man looking back.' 'I've become that man already,' Gene replies, 'I've had to be so that people round here can live their lives without the bastards pushing drugs on their families. Ruining lives.' Sam won't accept it. 'If you're that man then kill him,' he says, handing Gene a hammer that's been discarded. 'Go on –

if you're that man then you don't need anyone else: *you* do it.' Gene, seething, looks tempted for a moment, then throws the hammer through a window.

At the end, with Ravi recuperating in his hospital bed, Sam and Gene get drunk playing Thin Lizzy's 'Whisky in the Jar' to cheer him up.

■ **GENE MOMENT:** We discover more about Gene's past as he and Sam talk. 'I had a brother,' Gene tells him. 'Some bastard got him hooked on speed. I tried to knock sense into him, tried everything, haven't seen him in ten years. No one has. Can't change someone. It's like Chris, you put the effort in and what do you get? The same stupid grin. Stupid addict, didn't want to be helped.' 'You know addiction's usually a sign of something else missing from your life,' says Sam. 'Yeah,' Gene shrugs, 'but me and him were brought up exactly the same … *I'm* not addicted' He takes a big mouthful from his hip flask. 'I mean, you know the old man could be a bit loose with his fists when he'd had a jar or two, but by the time I was thirteen me and Stu together we could take him.' 'So, a happy childhood then…' Sam replies, not unkindly. 'It's tough losing someone.' 'Yeah… ' Gene has opened up enough. 'It was a long time ago, no need to come over all "Dorothy"'.

Later Sam offers to help Gene find his brother 'I already did, Sam,' Gene replies, 'just not in time.'

■ **FUTURE BLEED/MAYA:** This episode features the return of Sam's girlfriend Maya – whom he had to save from abduction in the first episode of series one. As the episode starts, Sam is dreaming of Maya by his hospital bed. 'Sam?' she says, 'I'm here, Sam. I hope you can hear me. I need to talk to you, Sam. I wish I could reach you.' When they arrive at the record shop he hears her voice again coming from a damaged police radio. 'I need to talk to you about something,' she says. 'Maya!' exclaims Sam. 'Sam? I sort of sensed you then… ' Maya replies on the radio. Sam is in shock that he might be able to communicate with her but the radio goes dead.

Later, Sam visits an Asian community centre and sees Maya appear as the heroine of a Bollywood movie. 'I don't know if you can hear me, Sam,' she says, 'but maybe it doesn't matter … I love you, Sam, but that's the trouble: when someone you love dies, you can say goodbye and go through all the stages you go through and move on. But you're still there, Sam, and nothing's getting better. I'm going to stop coming to see you, Sam. I'm sorry.' And later still she continues her farewell on Sam's TV screen, her voice coming from Prime Minister Edward Heath.

Finally when he visits a pregnant Layla in hospital – having realised that she is in fact Maya's mother – he looks at the tiny image on the ultrasound machine and whispers her name. 'That's a beautiful name,' says Layla and decides that's what she will call her daughter. 'Thanks for letting me go,' comes Maya's voice from the ultrasound. 'Goodbye, Sam.'

■ **SAM/ANNIE:** When Sam meets Annie outside the hospital room he tells her that 'there was unfinished business, but it's finished now…' He wants her to know that he is free and single. Mad as a hat-stand and convinced he's from the future, mark you, but at least he hasn't got a girlfriend. This pleases her immensely, which just goes to show how smitten she is, really…

■ **RAY MOMENT:** Yet again Ray proves he's a modern man by denying the suggestion that he's racist: 'Hey! I've got nothing against Gunga Dins!'

■ **DOUBLE MEANINGS:** It's strange for Sam when he and Layla visit Dipak in his coma: for once he's on the outside of this condition looking in. 'They said to play songs he liked…' Layla says, playing Elton John's 'Rocket Man' on a portable cassette player. 'Songs, voices, touch, anything familiar,' Sam says, looking at the prone body in its bed. 'How do you know?' Layla asks him. 'A friend?' Sam nods. 'Are they getting any better?' asks Layla. 'No… There's moments when people can sort of sense that he's still alive in there,' he replies.

Later, at Sam's flat, Layla says to Sam: 'Dipak was, you know … a stranger in a strange land. But you, Sam … it's like you've come from somewhere even further away.'

■ **HISTORICAL ROOTS (1):** Between August and December 1972 President Idi Amin forcibly expelled 80,000 Asians from Uganda. Around 30,000 of them came to Britain, many arriving penniless, having lost both homes and thriving businesses. The Heath government declared that Britain had a moral responsibility to help them, but several British cities felt otherwise, Leicester Council going so far as to advertise in Ugandan newspapers warning them not to come there – an act for which the city, with its now vibrant Asian community, has since formally apologized. But at the time many struggled against hostility and prejudice to make their lives successful, reflected by Ravi's anguished cry when he hears of his brother's murder: 'We came here to escape all this!'

■ **HISTORICAL ROOTS (2):** Knocked unconscious by Toolbox, Sam wakes up bound in ropes with an electric iron fixed to his chest. He struggles in panic but luckily the power cuts out. Power blackouts were a familiar part of life in 1973 as union action and low fuel stocks forced the government to implement the 'Three-Day Week', when hundreds of thousands of workers were laid off as commercial users were limited to three consecutive days of electrical use in order to try and eke out the ailing power supply.

■ **A BIT OF BOVVER:** The seventies saw plenty of action both by racists and anti-racists as the rise of the National Front was countered by the Anti-Nazi League and Rock Against Racism. Sam understandably loses it when he confronts a bunch of especially loutish skinheads painting slogans on a wall. 'What you doing, mate?' one objects, as Sam pulls out his warrant card, 'You're one of us.' 'What,' counters Sam, 'a dyslexic, racist moron?'

■ **MOVE OVER MR BRANSON:** Layla tells Sam that 'Dipak had a dream of owning a whole chain of record shops … enormous ones … like music supermarkets. He had a lot of crazy ideas.'

■ **BIN WATCH:** Three kissed by Cortina bumper at 1' 10".

impressed with Morgan and his methods: they are modern and similar to his own. Released under surveillance, Gene escapes and works with Sam to establish his innocence. 'I didn't do it, Sam,' Gene insists. 'I know,' Sam admits, 'it's proving it that's the problem.'

Between the two of them they piece together the missing hours of Gene's drunken bender, realising that Mackay was supposed to lose the fight that preceded his accident, and that it was Mackay who murdered Haslam and framed Gene.

■ **FUTURE BLEED:** Sam dreams about a phone that screams at him. The dream recurs and he hears what we will later realise to be the end of the next episode – Annie screaming as the shotguns fire.

EPISODE SEVEN

Gene is in court giving evidence against boxing manager Tony Haslam, whom he saw push his fighter Davie Mackay off a fire escape. The defence pleads that Mackay slipped; Mackay agrees and Haslam is found not guilty. Gene is furious. After a night of heavy drinking ends with Gene putting a brick through Haslam's window (losing his gun in the process), Sam is forced to leave him wandering the streets. He is later woken by a telephone call from Gene, who has got himself in trouble: 'I appear to have killed someone…' Haslam is dead and Gene has woken up next to the body with no idea how either he or Haslam got there.

Gene is taken into custody and the rest of CID are introduced to their new acting DCI: Frank Morgan, from *Hyde*. Sam can't help but be

■ **SAM/GENE:** Despite their frequent disagreements Gene has no doubt that Sam is the man to save him. When it comes to the investigation Gene is explicit: 'Just be the normal, picky, pain in the arse you usually are and I should be fine.'

Gene has also stopped taking backhanders: 'You know what really sticks in my gullet, what really burns?' he tells Sam, 'I stopped it. Months ago. You were right. Bring a villain down, bring him down *clean* and you feel like a hunter. King of your own jungle. Money can't buy that.'

■ **SAM/RAY:** After talking to Morgan in his office, Sam is stopped by Ray, who wants to know what the acting DCI is like. 'He seems very professional.' Sam admits. 'Bastard!' Ray replies, 'That's all we need.'

Later, in the Railway Arms, just as the fact that Gene might be guilty is starting to sink in, Ray lets some of his anger out on Sam: 'What I do regret is the day you walked on to my beat. Now, you may get to be my DCI but don't think for minute you'll get to be the tenth of the copper Gene Hunt was.'

■ **GENE MOMENT:** Exonerated, he stands before the gathered CID and makes a speech: 'I believe I have the right to feel a little upset. You see, I understood that I commanded your unswerving loyalty, love, affection and unquestioning obedience. Apparently I was mistaken. However, given the evidence with which you were confronted I can understand why that loyalty may have wavered. What I find *harder* to understand is how you miserable *tossers* could, for one second, believe that I could be a frigging bastard *murderer*.' He makes to walk into his office and then has another thought: 'Oh, and another thing, I should inform you that I intend to drink the equivalent of the North Sea in whisky tonight, so raid your piggy banks.'

■ **CHRIS MOMENT:** Chris's dancing makes Travolta look like, well … a really good dancer who would *never* stoop to such limb flailing ridiculousness. The poor lad looks like he's having a fit. It's a good job his mother loves him…

■ **ANNIE MOMENT:** Annie, under the orders of Frank Morgan who sees it as vital that the police should forge links with the community, must dress as Tufty the Road Safety Squirrel and visit schools. Gene later uses the costume to sneak into CID unrecognised.

■ **HISTORICAL ROOTS:** Created in 1953 by the late Elsie Mills MBE, Tufty Fluffytail featured in stories issued by the Royal Society for Prevention of Accidents instructing children on safety matters. The Tufty Under Fives club was launched in 1961 and went on to have 25,000 branches nationwide and two million members. Tufty is still fighting the good fight today, though he's ditched his frock coat and breeches for jeans and a T-shirt (sensible, given that were he to be seen in the former in some inner-city areas, he might wish a bus had hit him by the time the street-gangs had finished…)

■ **SAM/ANNIE:** CID is rollicking to the combination of music, Chris's dancing and the many gallons of booze that continue to flow. Annie, having had her fill, is stepping out of the office and towards the lift. Sam notices and catches her. 'Whoa…' he says, very drunk, 'where are you going?' 'Home,' she smiles. Sam doesn't want her to: a bit more to drink and he just might tell her how he feels. 'Stay,' he pleads. Annie changes the subject. 'You had to believe Gene was innocent, didn't you? Couldn't bear to think he might betray you.' 'Could you?' Sam

replies. 'Well,' Annie tells him, 'if you haven't got trust, who are you supposed to believe in?' 'You have to start with what you know, what you see in front of you,' says Sam. 'What do you see?' asks Annie. Sam is so close, he thinks so much of her: 'I see you.' They come together but Morgan appears and breaks the moment. Annie, flustered, carries on alone.

■ **HYDE CALLING:** Sam tries to call the number in Hyde but hears nothing but the sound of his own voice echoing back at him. At the end of the episode, though, facing Morgan, it becomes clear that his mysterious contact is close at hand. 'Hey, listen,' Sam says as Morgan is leaving, 'we're alright aren't we? You and me?' 'Oh yes…' Morgan replies with a smile, 'you're doing a great job.' 'Cheers,' says Sam. 'Really,' Morgan continues, 'we're all very proud of you. Not your fault Hunt wriggled out of it, good opportunity but …' he shrugs and steps into the lift. 'Hang in there Sam,' he says as he presses the button to descend, 'as soon as we can we'll sort this out. Bring you back home.'

EPISODE EIGHT

Life On Mars draws to a close as Sam is told that his body is about to be operated on in the future. Trying to do everything he can to guarantee the success of that operation he works with Frank Morgan to bring down Gene Hunt and his 'corrupt' department. Gene is giving him plenty of motivation too: the body of Danny Croucher is found, a miner who had got himself caught in the planning of a wages strike. Croucher had come to Hunt for help and Gene was happy to let him walk the streets in the hope of drawing out the blaggers. His negligence has caused Croucher's death.

Under duress, a known suspect, Danny Sykes, reveals the name of the man behind the planned robbery – Leslie Johns, career armed robber and cop killer – and Gene hatches a plot to go undercover and catch them in the act.

Following the investigation and informing on Gene to Morgan as he does so, Sam is torn between returning home and saving his friends as the undercover operation goes badly wrong and the guns start firing. Chris, panicking, is shot. Ray swiftly follows. The last thing Sam sees before he is enveloped by light and wakes up in his hospital room is Annie, trapped amid gunfire and in imminent danger of her life, begging him to help them.

At first all seems well, but as he tries to acclimatize to life back in the present day, the words of Nelson, the barman at the Railway Arms, return to haunt him: 'when you can *feel*, you're alive.' Sam doesn't feel. Not really. He has never felt so much a part of life as he did in his fantasy of 1973; the friends, the enemies and his love for Annie. All of that was more 'real' to him than his actual life.

He jumps from the roof of the police headquarters, returns to his friends and the gunfire, and saves the day. He has made his choice.

■ **FUTURE BLEED:** We open with Jimmy Savile on the radio: 'Alvin Stardust, hows about then? Wow! But the big news is they've found the cause of Sam's prolonged coma! Ooh! Now then guys and gals, there's a tumour in the temporal lobe of Sam's brain, they thought it was a clot but, hows about that, a clot it is not! Wow! It may be operable, double wow! Now then, as it happens, they need to know if Sam is strong enough for the operation; if he is, our very good friends here at the hospital say they can cut out the tumour.' Sam is grabbing the radio in both hands, elated at this: 'Cut it out! Cut it out! Fix it for me, Jim!'

Jimmy isn't listening but he has another surprise for Sam: 'Here is a request for the lad himself, from the gorgeous Ruth Tyler.' Sam hears his mum, begging him not to stop fighting as the surgeon, Mr Morgan, thinks this will be the best opportunity they have. *Morgan* … the phone rings and there he is, the fictional counterpart of the surgeon operating on him. Sam must destroy Gene Hunt and his department, insists Morgan, a theme that continues throughout the first half of the episode. 'He's out of control, Sam,' says 1973 Morgan about Gene, 'like a cancer; the sooner we cut him out…' Sam knows the answer: '… the sooner I can leave.' Morgan then repeats the need for Sam to be strong.

Preparations for the operation constantly bleed through: he hears a nurse's voice in Lost and Found announcing that he is ready for his pre-medication and later his TV set turns into an ECG monitor showing his heart-rate. When he begins to wake up, the railway tunnel he is stood in floods with light – alluding to the

many references of those who have suffered from 'near-death' experiences witnessing a tunnel of light. Finally, having returned to his 1973 fantasy world of his own volition he hears the last, pointless voice of a paramedic on the Cortina radio. 'Its no good,' it says, 'he's slipping away from us. Sam…? Sam…?' Sam switches it off: he has had quite enough of the future.

■ **HISTORICAL NOTE:** Sir James Wilson Vincent Savile OBE is one of the UK's most recognisable personalities. One-time professional wrestler he became famous as a Radio DJ in the sixties and presented seminal BBC chart show *Top of the Pops* when it was first aired in 1964. He was the co-host of the show for its final episode in 2006. He presented his own programme, *Jim'll Fix It*, between 1975 and 1994 where viewers could write in with their wishes – which varied from the trivial to the life-changing – and have them granted by the cigar-toting, jewellery-encrusted, tracksuit-wearing Fairy Godmother that was Jim. After having had their dream come true he would present them with a medal which stated, 'Jim fixed it for me'.

■ **RED HERRING:** An unexpected twist thrown at us in this episode is the momentary doubt that maybe 1973 was more real than we thought. Claiming that Sam is suffering from amnesia, DCI Morgan takes him to visit the graves of his parents, telling him that his real name is Sam Williams of C Division, Hyde, and that his parents, David and Brenda, died in a coach crash when he was twelve (an accident that sent the young Sam into a 'waking coma' for some weeks). Sam remembers a crash when he was twelve in which he broke his arm, throwing more confusion into the mix. In the same graveyard they see the headstones of Vic and Ruth Tyler, then that of Sam Tyler himself, all allegedly where he and Morgan got the inspiration for Sam's cover story. To top it off, Morgan wonders whether the amnesia and disorientation were caused by the car accident Sam had on the way to his assignment at A Division. Sam doesn't know what to believe any more – and neither do we. Tormented by the possibilities, Sam returns to the CID office and hunts out his transfer file with Morgan's signature. Could this all be real? If so then he is about to betray everyone… He is desperate for signs of the future, noises, visions … anything. But they don't come.

■ **SAM/GENE:** The struggle that has played out between Sam and Gene over the two series goes from one extreme to the other in this episode. Initially Sam is determined to see himself rid of Gene, revolted by his methods which have caused the death of Danny Croucher and the torture of Danny Sykes which leads to the team being put in mortal danger. The clash of styles is at its most pronounced: 'Grab 'em by the balls and their hearts and minds will surely follow,' says Gene, '*that* is policing.' 'Our definitions of policing may vary marginally,' Sam sighs. 'And yours is?' asks Gene. Sam's reply is instant: 'Serve the public trust, protect the innocent, uphold the law.' 'Training college?' Gene assumes. Sam has learned his methods from a much nobler source, though: '*Robocop*.'

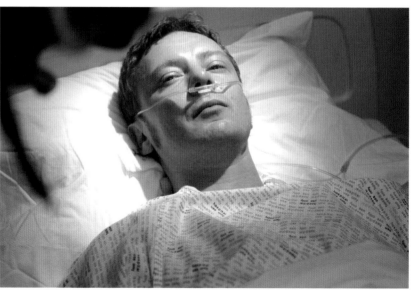

These are two men who are worlds apart. Later when Sam is recording Gene's plan of action, the tape recorder is hidden beneath a porno magazine. 'This my copy of *Just Jugs*?' Gene asks, spotting it on the desk as he leaves. 'Yeah,' Sam admits, nervously slapping his hand on it, terrified that Gene will pick it up and see the tape recorder. 'It is.' 'What are you doing with it?' Gene wants to know. 'There's an interview with Kingsley Amis in it that I really want to read,' is

bullets and broken glass flew – that he wouldn't leave her. At the end Sam stands outside the Railway Arms with her and they finally get their moment. 'What should I do, Annie?' he asks her. 'Stay here forever,' she replies. Sam smiles, 'Alright then.' And (in the words of the intensely romantic scene directions in Matthew Graham's shooting script) he "snogs her face off with two series' worth of built-up passion."

Sam's quick reply. 'You know,' Gene sighs, 'the saddest thing is I *believe* you.'

Morgan wants Sam to prove that Gene is guilty of serious professional misconduct. 'That shouldn't be too hard,' Sam comments. Still, as he begins to doubt himself, he gets cold feet. He and Gene have been through a lot together. When he starts to suspect that the world of 1973 may be real he realizes that to betray Gene and have him pensioned off would kill him. Can he do it?

■ **SAM/ANNIE:** Finally their feelings for one another become clear and are mutually expressed. Accepting that he will soon be gone, Sam opens up to Annie, insisting that they both knew he didn't belong there. He even asks her to spend the night with him, 'just once, no questions, no answers, just you and me.' Annie can't, not if she knows it's only for one night. As much as she feels for him she wants more than that.

When Sam admits to her that he is working undercover to catch Gene she is beside herself, slapping him – hard – and storming out in tears. It is for Annie, more than anything else, that he returns to his fantasy. He promised her – as the

■ **PROMISES, PROMISES:** Before he makes the momentous decision to leave the present once and for all, Sam, thinking of his pledge to Annie not to leave her, tells his mother: 'I made a promise to someone.' 'Then they've got nothing to worry about,' his mum reassures him, 'cos you always keep your promises.'

■ **DOUBLE MEANINGS:** You can't move for double meanings in the final episode. From the mirroring of Sam's real operation and the undercover mission for Morgan to little details like his conversation with Annie ('You should see a doctor' she tells him. 'That's a good idea,' he replies) the whole episode plays out – as it should – as a veritable smorgasbord of metaphor.

■ **GOD IS IN THE DETAILS:** The episode has many fine details for the eagle-eyed viewer, including the many *Wizard of Oz* references (see interview with SJ Clarkson). We see again the sign advertising 'Hyde's Anvil Stout'; Sam's hospital room is revealed as number 2612, Hyde Ward – the telephone number and area

he hailed from in his fantasy – and when Sam is dictating his notes for psychological evaluation after his recovery from the operation he repeats the voiceover from the series titles almost word for word. Possibly the cheekiest reference is the splendidly jargon-loaded title of DCI Morgan's policing scheme, under which he and Sam are ostensibly working to bring Gene down: it rejoices in the name of the Metropolitan Accountability and Reconciliation Strategy (M.A.R.S.)

■ **CHRIS MOMENT:** 'Undercover…' says Chris as he, Ray and Sam spy on Leslie Johns, '… stake-outs and that. This is what I signed up for.' 'It's not the Famous Five.' Sam mutters. 'Oh, don't spoil it, Boss,' Chris complains.

He stands up to Sam when it's revealed that he's been undercover all along, however. 'I looked up to you, Boss,' he says before storming out (smashing a phone as he goes). By the end, of course, they are reconciled. Chris apologizes for his outburst and Sam tells him he's going to be a good copper. Chris is over the moon at such praise, until something occurs to him: 'What do you mean, *going* to be?'

■ **RAY MOMENT:** Ray has more than enough evidence in this episode to persuade him that

his opinion of Sam has been right all along. 'He's never stood shoulder to shoulder with us and he never will,' he tells Chris; and when Sam's undercover mission is exposed, Ray is gratified Sam is revealed as the 'enemy', something he had always been convinced of. Come the end, however, Sam is forgiven somewhat. That Ray met a nurse with an arse like 'two Cox's Pippins in a bag' while having his gunshot wound treated has to have helped…

There's no doubt, though, that Sam and Ray could never be friends. They're from different worlds. 'Ray, you up to a bit of playacting?' Gene asks while detailing the plan to nab Leslie Johns. 'Doddle, Guv. It's not *Hamlet*,' Ray replies. 'Good,' is Sam's rejoinder, 'because *Hamlet* is a tragedy.' 'Trust you to know that,' Ray mutters, 'poof.'

■ **TEST CARD GIRL:** The Test Card Girl appears twice in the final episode: once when she stands bathed in red light outside the door of Sam's flat. 'Knock knock,' she says as he falls to the floor. He sees flashes of Annie screaming and the sound of shotguns as the events of the future pre-shadow themselves. Then, right at the end, she appears at the end of a row of dancing children, looks straight at us and then 'turns off' the picture.

LOST AND FOUND:
THE LAST TRAIN...

It was dark and somewhere there was the sound of glass breaking.

'Watch yourself,' Adams whispered. 'Sounds like they're just up ahead.'

Thompson put his hand against the wall to steady himself. He felt sick. 'Who's up ahead?'

'The train robbers, obviously!'

Thompson's stomach heaved and he dropped to his haunches. Train robbers ... oh, good. There was something distinctly wrong with all of this. 'Last thing I remember, we were in the car with Gene.'

Adams crept over to him. 'Eh? That was ages ago, mate. We dropped him off at the gym and then found out all about it later, as per bloody usual, sat here on the sidelines.'

'It wasn't ages ago, it was just now. And before that I was in a hospital with DS Carling... Then the pub... It's all getting weird. What's happening to us? I just want to wake up. Back in the present day, back in the real world.'

'Yeah...' Adams wasn't really listening. He'd found something on the floor of the railway tunnel. Flicking his cigarette lighter, he lit up the cover of a garish-looking comic book. '*Life On Mars*!' the title read. 'Cool...' he whispered.

A shotgun fired ahead. The sound of screaming. More shots.

Thompson's head was splitting. He could hear the gunfire but was unable to look up. 'We shouldn't even be here, it's all just in our heads. We need to wake up. Stay here any longer and anything could happen...'

'Look at this though. You'll never guess what! Look who that is...' Adams pushed the comic towards Thompson and suddenly the tunnel was filled with light.

Light and the sound of someone shouting...

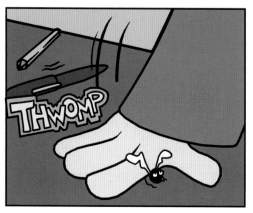

SOMETIMES OUR IMAGINATIONS CAN BE A BETTER PLACE TO LIVE.

NORT[H] WEST DIST[RICT]

Co-Created By
Matthew Graham
Tony Jordan
Ashley Pharoah

CASE FILE

SERIES TWO EPISODE ONE

WRITTEN BY MATTHEW GRAHAM
PRODUCED BY CAMERON ROACH
DIRECTED BY SJ CLARKSON

DCI GENE HUNT	PHILIP GLENISTER
DI SAM TYLER	JOHN SIMM
DS RAY CARLING	DEAN ANDREWS
DC CHRIS SKELTON	MARSHALL LANCASTER
WDC ANNIE CARTWRIGHT	LIZ WHITE
WPC PHYLLIS DOBBS	NOREEN KERSHAW

In the present day, Sam is being threatened while he sleeps. He sees a shadowy figure by his bedside and hears a familiar voice whisper promises of violence in his ears.

In 1973 a murder on a bus leads Gene and Sam to investigate casino boss Tony Crane. Sam knows Crane from the future, knows the monster he will become. He begins to realize that this is who is threatening him in the future. Can Sam prove that Tony Crane is the man they're looking for? Solve a crime in the past to prevent the deaths of those in the future - himself included.

ARE YOU FEELING LUCKY?

by a staff reporter

Vagas-style glamour coming to town as The Wild Card Club opens today in the heart of Manchetser. Whilst the new venue is far from Manchetser's first gambling house, The Wild Club Manager Tony Crane, pictured with his staff of croupiers (left), emphasized that his enterprise will revolutionize the face of casino culture in the city.

Pictured above Tony Crane The Wild Card Club Manager at the launch

Original Broadcast Stats
Run Time: 58' 59"
Transmission: Tuesday 13th February 2007, 9pm BBC ONE

Viewing Figures for original broadcast:
Overnight Ratings: 5.7 million
Adjusted Ratings: 6.4 million
Audience Share: 23.2%

Adjusted figures include time-shift recordings.

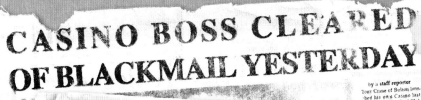

CASINO BOSS CLEARED
OF BLACKMAIL YESTERDAY

by a staff reporter
Tony Crane of Bolton launched his own Casino last
night. The Wild Card Club
...running high

FRAUD CHARGES
SUDDENLY DROPPED

by a staff reporter
Tony Crane of Bolton launched his own Casino last
night. The Wild Card Club
already running high
between fans of the
city's two football
teams.
This murder is the
latest in a number of
football related
incidents which have
occured in the
Manchester Area. On
Wednesday of last
week, four youths...
taken...

THE CHIPS ARE U|

by a staff reporter
Tony Crane of Bolton launched his own Casino last
night. The Wild Card Club.
already running high
between fans of the
city's two football
teams.
This murder is the
latest in a number of
football related
incidents which have
occured in the
Manchester Area. On
Wednesday of last
week, four youths were
taken into Police
custody after being
caught painting
slogans onto the
outside of the Old
Trafford football
stadium.

The Wild Card Club just yesterday evening

Head In The Sky - Atomic Rooster
Street Life - Roxy Music
Break Through - Atomic Rooster
Son of My Father - Chicory Tip
Everybody Gets to Go to the Moon - The Three Degrees
Spooky - Dusty Springfield
Year of Decision - The Three Degrees
Star Man - David Bowie

INT. THE WILD CARD CLUB - NIGHT 1/1 20:15

Lava lamps. Feel of the harem to it. SAM
strides in closely followed by GENE. SAM
is still fighting a sense of forboding.

                    GENE
        Routine interviews and you're giving
        Crane the third degree.
                    SAM
        Yeah well take a man like Crane.
        Young. Prodigious. Ruthless. He's
        running illegal card houses by 28...
        and in those places you'll find more
        rigging than HMS Victory.
                    GENE
        All casino bosses have a past
                    SAM
        Somebody like Tony Crane does not
        rise so fast without getting blood
        on his hands. And as for where he's
        heading...
                    GENE
        Sounds like a vendetta. Was he
        boffing your kid sister up the harris
        and eating all your cream horns
        while he was at it?

NELSON	TONY MARSHALL		
TONY CRANE	MARC WARREN		
REPORTER	JONATHAN WRIGHT		
HARRY WOOLF	KEVIN R MCNALLY		
RUSSELL ASKEY	CRAIG CHEETHAM		
ANDY EDDOWS	STEVE GARTI		
EVE OLAWI	YASMIN BANNERMAN		
MCKEE	MICHAEL ATKINSON		
DOCTOR	JULIAN KAY		
NURSE	GEMMA WARDLE		

Tony Crane
(AKA Marc Warren)

Previous Form:
Hustle
Band of Brothers
Doctor Who
State of Play
Grange Hill

Stunt Co-ordinators	Peter Brayham	Production Buyer	Ron Pritchard
Stunt Performers	Guy List	Props Master	Peter O'Rourke
	Matthew Stirling	Prop Hands	Jim Mate
	Derek Lea		Greg White
	Gordon Seed	Standby Props	Gary Leech
	Dani Biernat	Standby Props	Paula Barrington
1st Assistant Director	Jonathan Leather	Standby Carpenter	Gary McCabe
2nd Assistant Director	Andi Coldwell	Construction Manager	Chris Watson
3rd Assistant Director	Chantelle Stoffel	Costume Supervisor	Becky Davies
Floor Runner	Jack Casey	Costume Assistant	Alison Cook
Production Co-ordinator	Tracey Lee Staple		Amanda Crossley
Assistant Co-ordinator	Samantha Milnes	Make-up Supervisor	Debbie Salmon
Production Office Runner	Danielle Eglin	Make-up Artist	Amanda Isaacs
Continuity	Angie Pontefract	Make-up Assistant	Jenny Ward
	Steve Walker	Post Prod. Supervisor	Jessica Rundle
Development Script Editor	Kerry Appleyard	Assistant Editor	Penny Clark
Police Advisor	Steve Crimmins	Online Editors	Scott Hinchcliffe
Production Accountant	Diane Pontefract		James Osborne
Assistant Accountant	Matthew Pope	Colourist	Jet Omoshebi
Location Manager	Brett Wilson	Dialogue Editor	Alex Sawyer
Asst. Location Manager	Joseph Cairns	Effects Editor	Darren Banks
Unit Manager	Karen Milner	Re-Recording Mixer	James Feltham
Camera Operator	Nick Beek-Sanders	Titles	Why Not Associates
Focus Puller	Steve Smith	Visual Effects Supervisor	Matt Wood
Clapper Loader	Kim Tunstall	Publicity	Premier PR
Camera Assistant	Danny Mendieta	BBC Production Exec	Julie Scott
Grip	Robin Stone	Script Editor	Gabriel Silver
Boom Operator	Paul Watson	Sound Recordist	Dave Sansom
Sound Assistant	Anthony Hurst	Make-up & Hair Designer	Emma White
Gaffer	Brian Jones	Costume Designer	Emma Rosenthal
Best Boy	Terry Eden	Casting Director	David Shaw
Electrician	Danny Griffiths	Production Designer	Matthew Gant
	Vinny Cowper	Music By	Edmund Butt
Genny Operator	Tony O'Brien	Editor	Sarah Brewerton
Art Director	Tom Still	Director of Photography	Balazs Bolygo
Standby Art Director	Dan Taylor	Co-Producer	Marcus Wilson
Art Dept Assistant	Andy Hare	Executive Producers	Jane Featherstone
			Claire Parker
			Matthew Graham

NORT...
DIST...

CASE FILE

SERIES TWO
EPISODE TWO

Co-Created By
Matthew Graham
Tony Jordan
Ashley Pharoah

WRITTEN BY CHRIS CHIBNALL
PRODUCED BY CAMERON ROACH
DIRECTED BY SJ CLARKSON

DCI GENE HUNT	PHILIP GLENISTER
DI SAM TYLER	JOHN SIMM
DS RAY CARLING	DEAN ANDREWS
DC CHRIS SKELTON	MARSHALL LANCASTER
WDC ANNIE CARTWRIGHT	LIZ WHITE
WPC PHYLLIS DOBBS	NOREEN KERSHAW

After a long-running spate of armed robberies, DCI Gene Hunt orders the release from prison of safe-cracker 'Dickie Fingers' for interrogation.

While escorting Fingers from Prison, Sam, Chris and Ray are held up by armed men and Fingers is abducted.

Gene's friend and mentor Superintendent Harry Woolf joins the investigation, determined to bring the long criminal career of Arnold Malone - the man he believes to be responsible - to an end.

As the investigation continues, however, it appears that all may not be so simple, and the culprit is closer to home than any of them suspect...

MUSIC

Original Broadcast Stats
Run Time: 57' 57"
Transmission: Tuesday 20th February 2007,
              9pm BBC ONE

Viewing Figures for BBC ONE broadcast:
  Overnight Ratings: 5.7 million
  Adjusted Ratings: 6.1 million
  Audience Share: 23.5%

Adjusted figures include time-shift recordings.

Sweet Jane - Mott The Hoople
In The Summertime - Mungo Jerry
Ain't Got No performed - Derek Wadsworth from Hair
Love Machine - Uriah Heep
Bird Of Prey - Uriah Heep
Long Cool Woman In A Black Dress - The Hollies
Goodbye Yellow Brick Road - Elton John

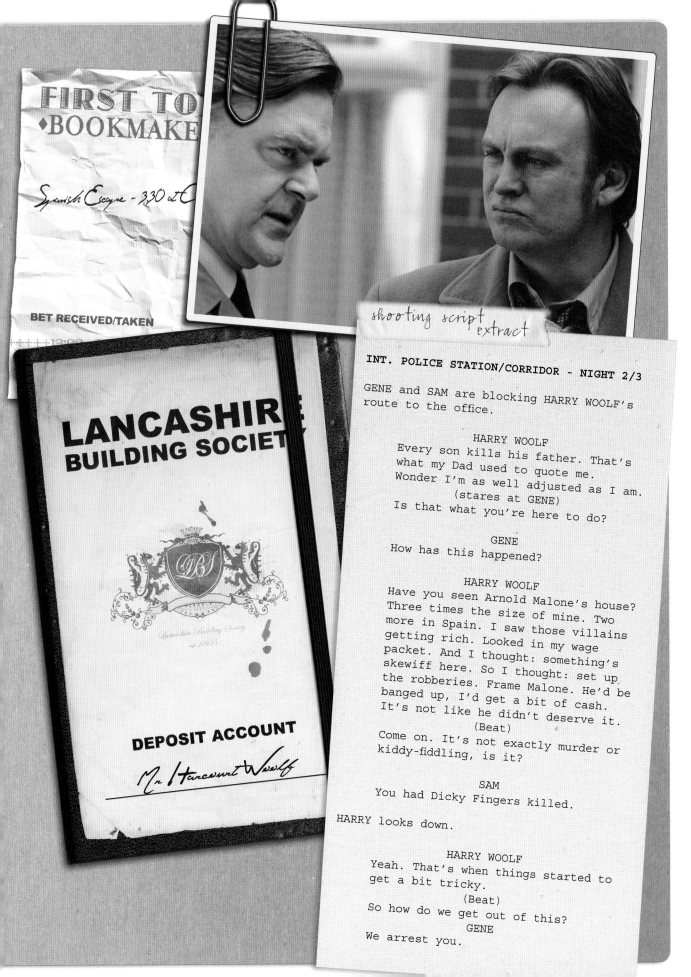

FIRST TO
♦BOOKMAKE

Spanish Escayne - 330 at C

BET RECEIVED/TAKEN

LANCASHIRE
BUILDING SOCIETY

Lancashire Building Society
est 1803

DEPOSIT ACCOUNT

Mr Harcourt Woolf

shooting script extract

INT. POLICE STATION/CORRIDOR - NIGHT 2/3

GENE and SAM are blocking HARRY WOOLF's route to the office.

HARRY WOOLF
Every son kills his father. That's what my Dad used to quote me.
Wonder I'm as well adjusted as I am.
(stares at GENE)
Is that what you're here to do?

GENE
How has this happened?

HARRY WOOLF
Have you seen Arnold Malone's house? Three times the size of mine. Two more in Spain. I saw those villains getting rich. Looked in my wage packet. And I thought: something's skewiff here. So I thought: set up the robberies. Frame Malone. He'd be banged up, I'd get a bit of cash. It's not like he didn't deserve it.
(Beat)
Come on. It's not exactly murder or kiddy-fiddling, is it?

SAM
You had Dicky Fingers killed.

HARRY looks down.

HARRY WOOLF
Yeah. That's when things started to get a bit tricky.
(Beat)
So how do we get out of this?
GENE
We arrest you.

HARRY WOOLF	KEVIN R MCNALLY
DICKIE FINGERS	STEVE EVETS
1ST TWIN	CHRIS BIESKE
2ND TWIN	CRAIG BIESKE
DC GLEN FLETCHER	RAY EMMET BROWN
FILBERT	BILL RODGERS
ARNOLD MALONE	STEPHEN BENT
ARMED ROBBER	TREVOR WILIAMS

Supt. Harry Woolf
(AKA Kevin McNally)

Previous Form:
 Pirates of the Caribbean
 Johnny English
 De-Lovely
 Spice World
 Doctor Who

Stunt Co-ordinator	Peter Brayham
Stunt Performers	Derek Lea
	Gordon Seed
	Crispin Layfield
	Paul Howell
	Chris Newton
1st Assistant Director	Jonathan Leather
2nd Assistant Director	Andi Coldwell
3rd Assistant Director	Chantelle Stoffel
Floor Runner	Jack Casey
Production Co-ordinator	Tracy Lee Sapple
Assistant Co-ordinator	Samantha Milnes
Production Office Runner	Danielle Eglin
Continuity	Angie Pontefract
	Steve Walker
Police Advisor	Steve Crimmins
Production Accountant	Diane Pontefract
Assistant Accountant	Matthew Pope
Location Manager	Brett Wilson
Asst Location Manager	Joseph Cairns
Unit Manager	Karen Milner
Camera Operator	Nick Beek-Sanders
Focus Puller	Steve Smith
Clapper Loader	Kim Tunstall
Camera Assistant	Danny Mendieta
Grip	Robin Stone
Boom Operator	Paul Watson
Sound Assistant	Anthony Hurst
Gaffer	Brian Jones
Best Boy	Terry Eden
Electrician	Danny Griffiths
	Vinny Cowper
Genny Operator	Tony O'Brien
Art Director	Tom Still
Standby Art Director	Dan Taylor
Art Dept Assistant	Andy Hare
Production Buyer	Ron Pritchard
Props Master	Peter O'Rourke
Prop Hands	Jim Mate
	Marcus Holt
Standby Props	Gary Leech
	Paula Barrington

Standby Carpenter	Gary McCabe
Construction Manager	Chris Watson
Costume Supervisor	Becky Davies
Costume Assistant	Alison Cook
	Amanda Crossley
Make-up Supervisor	Debbie Salmon
Make-up Artist	Amanda Isaacs
Make-Up Assistant	Jenny Ward
Post Prod. Supervisor	Jessica Rundle
Assistant Editor	Penny Clark
Online Editors	Scott Hinchcliffe
	James Osborne
Colourist	Jet Omoshebi
Dialogue Editor	Alex Sawyer
Effects Editor	Darren Banks
Re-Recording Mixer	James Feltham
Titles	Why Not Associates
Publicity	Premier PR
BBC Production Exec	Julie Scott
Script Editor	Gabriel Silver
Sound Recordist	Dave Sansom
Make-up & Hair Designer	Emma White
Costume Designer	Emma Rosenthal
Casting Director	David Shaw
Production Designer	Matthew Gant
Music By	Edmund Butt
Editor	Sarah Brewerton
Director of Photography	Balazs Bolygo
Co-Producer	Marcus Wilson
Executive Producers	Jane Featherstone
	Claire Parker
	Matthew Graham

Co-Created By
Matthew Graham
Tony Jordan
Ashley Pharoah

...WEST
...T C.I.D

CASE FILE

SERIES TWO
EPISODE THREE

WRITTEN BY JULIE RUTTERFORD
PRODUCED BY CAMERON ROACH
DIRECTED BY RICHARD CLARK

DCI GENE HUNT	PHILIP GLENISTER
DI SAM TYLER	JOHN SIMM
DS RAY CARLING	DEAN ANDREWS
DC CHRIS SKELTON	MARSHALL LANCASTER
WDC ANNIE CARTWRIGHT	LIZ WHITE
WPC PHYLLIS DOBBS	NOREEN KERSHAW

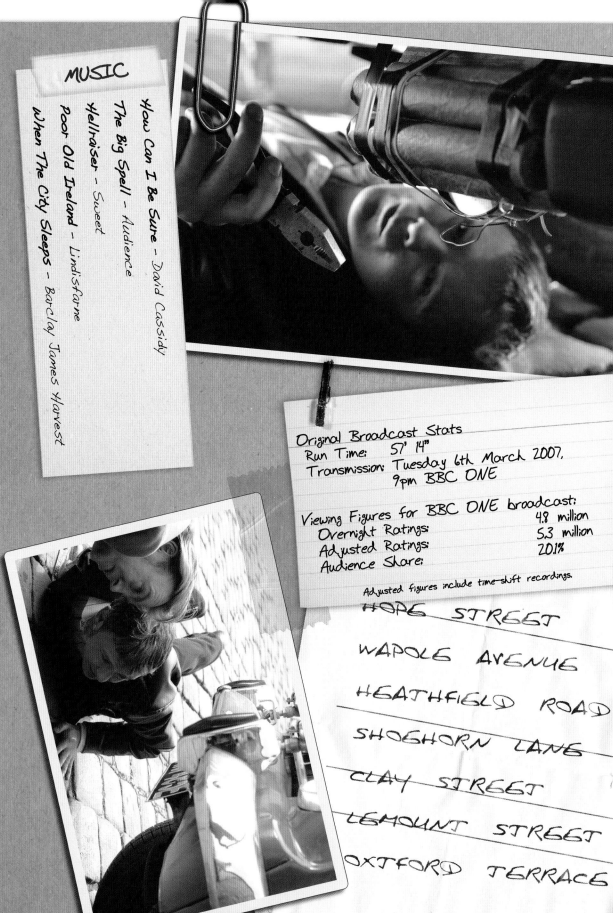

Original Broadcast Stats

Run Time: 57' 14"

Transmission: Tuesday 6th March 2007,
9pm BBC ONE

Viewing Figures for BBC ONE broadcast:

Overnight Ratings: 4.8 million

Adjusted Ratings: 5.3 million

Audience Share: 20.1%

Adjusted figures include time-shift recordings.

HOPE STREET

WAPOLE AVENUE

HEATHFIELD ROAD

SHOGHORN LANE

CLAY STREET

LEMOUNT STREET

OXTFORD TERRACE

A car bomb is reported to A Division: allegedly the work of the IRA.

After Sam's conviction that the bomb is a hoax nearly costs DS Carling his life, he must work on his own to prove the bomber is no terrorist.

With the Irish community under attack from a desperate police force, Sam knows that they will have a riot on their hands unless he can get to the truth of what's going on.

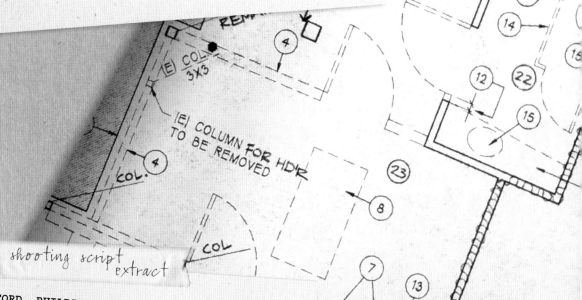

shooting script extract

EXT. SALFORD. BUILDING SITE/YARD. DAY 3/2 - 1212.

                    MILLER
         (low voice) Maybe don't let on it was me who
    called you? It's mainly Irish fellas work for
    me and I don't want them getting the wrong end
    of the stick - I rely on them a lot.
                    GENE
    Don't worry, Frank, discretion's our middle
    name...

CUT TO: GENE and SAM with a group of IRISH WORKERS.

                    GENE
    Top of the morning to you, lads. Know anything
    about some missing dynamite?

SAM looks at GENE - subtle as a sledgehammer.

NELSON　　　TONY MARSHALL
PATRICK O'BRIEN　　BRENDAN MACKEY
FRANK MILLER　　PETER WIGHT
LANDLADY　　BEATRICE KELLEY
TEST CARD GIRL　　HARRIET ROGERS

Patrick O'Brien
(AKA Brendan Mackey)

Previous Form:
Touching The Void
9 Dead Gay Guys
Boxed
H3
Always and Everyone

Stunt Co-ordinator	Peter Brayham
Stunt Performers	Ray Nicholas
	Tim Halloran
	Dean Forster
	Gordon Seed
1st Assistant Director	Martin Curry
2nd Assistant Director	Andi Coldwell
3rd Assistant Director	Chantelle Stoffel
Floor Runner	Jack Casey
Production Co-ordinator	Tracy Lee Sapple
Assistant Co-ordinator	Samantha Milnes
Production Office Runner	Danielle Eglin
Continuity	Angie Pontefract
	Steve Walker
Police Advisor	Steve Crimmins
Production Accountant	Diane Pontefract
Assistant Accountant	Matthew Pope
Location Manager	Brett Wilson
Asst. Location Manager	Joseph Cairns
Location Assistant	Georgie Turnbull
Camera Operator	Nick Beek-Sanders
Focus Puller	Steve Smith
Clapper Loader	Kim Tunstall
Camera Assistant	Danny Mendieta
Grip	Robin Stone
Boom Operator	Paul Watson
Sound Assistant	Anthony Hurst
Gaffer	Brian Jones
Best Boy	Terry Eden
Electrician	Danny Griffiths
	Vinny Cowper
Genny Operator	Tony O'Brien
Art Director	Tom Still
Standby Art Director	Dan Taylor
Art Dept Assistant	Andy Hare
Production Buyer	Ron Pritchard
Props Master	Peter O'Rourke
Prop Hands	Jim Mate
	Marcus Holt
Standby Props	Gary Leech
	Neil O'Rourke
Standby Carpenter	Gary McCabe

Construction Manager	Chris Watson
Costume Supervisor	Becky Davies
Costume Assistant	Alison Cook
	Amanda Crossley
Make-up Supervisor	Debbie Salmon
Make-up Artist	Amanda Isaacs
Make-Up Assistant	Jenny Ward
Post Prod. Supervisor	Jessica Rundle
Assistant Editor	Penny Clark
Online Editors	Scott Hinchcliffe
	James Osborne
Colourist	Jet Omoshebi
Dialogue Editor	Alex Sawyer
Effects Editor	Darren Banks
Re-Recording Mixer	James Feltham
Titles	Why Not Associates
Visual Effects Supervisor	Simon Blackledge
Publicity	Premier PR
Music Advisors	Blind Beggar Ltd.
BBC Production Exec	Julie Scott
Script Editor	Gabriel Silver
Sound Recordist	Dave Sansom
Make-up & Hair Designer	Emma White
Costume Designer	Emma Rosenthal
Casting Director	David Shaw
Production Designer	Matthew Gant
Music By	Edmund Butt
Editor	Jeremy Stachan
Director of Photography	Balazs Bolygo
Co-Producer	Marcus Wilson
Executive Producers	Jane Featherstone
	Claire Parker
	Matthew Graham

NORTH WEST DISTRICT C.I.D

Co-Created By
Matthew Graham
Tony Jordan
Ashley Pharoah

WRITTEN BY ASHLEY PHAROAH
PRODUCED BY CAMERON ROACH
DIRECTED BY RICHARD CLARK

CASE FILE

SERIES TWO
EPISODE FOUR

DCI GENE HUNT	PHILIP GLENISTER
DI SAM TYLER	JOHN SIMM
DS RAY CARLING	DEAN ANDREWS
DC CHRIS SKELTON	MARSHALL LANCASTER
WDC ANNIE CARTWRIGHT	LIZ WHITE
WPC PHYLLIS DOBBS	NOREEN KERSHAW

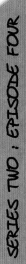

Lay Down by The Strawbs replaced with Story in Your Eyes by The Moody Blues for international and DVD releases.

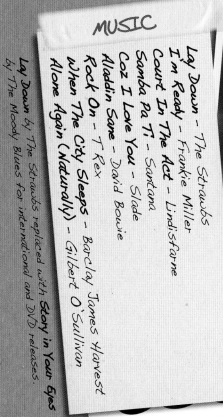

MUSIC

Lay Down - The Strawbs
I'm Ready - Frankie Miller
Court In The Act - Lindisfarne
Samba Pa Ti - Santana
Coz I Love You - Slade
Aladdin Sane - David Bowie
Rock On - T Rex
When The City Sleeps - Barclay James Harvest
Alone Again (Naturally) - Gilbert O'Sullivan

eauvoir
Catalogue 1973

shooting script extract

INT - MORTUARY - DAY 4/2 1700

SAM and GENE look on as the PATHOLOGIST finishes expecting
the dead woman on the slab.
                          PATHOLOGIST
    Cause of death would appear to be a blow to the head.
    Possibly struck against a wall or kerb
                          GENE

Raped?
                          PATHOLOGIST
    Hard to say. There was one thing that might
    interest you, DCI Hunt
                          GENE

What?
                          PATHOLOGIST
    (In french) La fleur de mort.
                          GENE
    I once hit a man for speaking French.

Original Broadcast Stats

Run Time: 58' 37"
Transmission: Tuesday 13th March 2007,
                 9pm BBC ONE

Viewing Figures for original broadcast:
  Overnight Ratings: 5.1 million
  Adjusted Ratings: 5.3 million
  Audience Share: 21.4%
        Adjusted figures include time-shift recordings.

All th
right a

The body of a young woman is found in a piece of waste-ground. Sam's memories of his childhood are triggered as both the victim and his Aunt Heather were Beauvoir beauty reps.

After trying to teach A Division modern surveillance methods, Sam goes undercover with Gene and Annie in swinging suburbia on the hunt for the killer.

Santana plays on the turntable while vol-au-vents are washed down with Blue Nun. Before you know it the car keys are on the table and the wife swapping is about to begin

Hannington

Dear Tony and Cherie Blair,

Allow me, as club secretary to officially welcome you to Hannington's Tennis Club and to extend my si... you both very much enjoy your member... winning courts (we have been awarded t... Grass" Award two years running and our... flexing their green fingers to ensure t... is announced next month) we also pride... facilities. Bunny's Bar has a particular... well as a full range of wines and spirits... selection that you may wish to sip as a d... all those volleys and lobs. Every year we... to feel is the must attend New Year Party... our, always delicious, buffet we like to la... entertainment (this year The Grumbleweeds... aisles, an up and coming music and comedy... to book next year too).

Attached is a reminder of our Accept... I have no doubt will be no more than a forma... the Fison s award without making sure every... Proper Pump Policy).

I look forward to seeing you both with us soon and, who knows, maybe we could even partner up for a round of doubles? Though I should warn you that my wife, Jennifer, has a very strong wrist and has brought many a man gasping to their knees

Yours Faithfully,

Alexander Martin

Alexander Martin
Club Secretary

ROGER TWILLING	NICHOLAS PALLISER
CAROL TWILLING	EVA POPE
MRS LUCKHURST	CLARE MCGLINN
DENISE WILLIAMS	GEORGIA TAYLOR
AUNTIE HEATHER	KATHERINE KELLY
PATHOLOGIST	ANDY HOCKLEY
MRS EDITH WILLIAMS	MERYL HAMPTON
TWILLING'S LAWYER	ANDREW READMAN
YOUNG SAM	ALEXANDER O'LOUGHLIN
PROFESSOR	RICHARD SINNOTT
GRACIE	CARISSA WISTOW

Denise Williams
(AKA Georgia Taylor)

Previous Form:
  The History Boys
  Blackpool
  The Royal
  Where The Heart Is
  Coronation Street

Stunt Co-ordinator	Peter Brayham			
Stunt Performers	Tracy Caudle			
	Stuart Clark		Construction Manager	Chris Watson
1st Assistant Director	Martin Curry		Costume Supervisor	Becky Davies
2nd Assistant Director	Andi Coldwell		Costume Assistant	Alison Cook
3rd Assistant Director	Chantelle Stoffel			Amanda Crossley
Floor Runner	Jack Casey		Make-up Supervisor	Debbie Salmon
Production Co-ordinator	Tracy Lee Sapple		Make-up Artist	Amanda Isaacs
Assistant Co-ordinator	Samantha Milnes		Make-Up Assistant	Jenny Ward
Production Office Runner	Danielle Eglin		Post Prod. Supervisor	Jessica Rundle
Continuity	Angie Pontefract		Assistant Editor	Penny Clark
	Steve Walker		Online Editors	Scott Hinchcliffe
Police Advisor	Steve Crimmins			James Osborne
Production Accountant	Diane Pontefract		Colourist	Jet Omoshebi
Assistant Accountant	Matthew Pope		Dialogue Editor	Alex Sawyer
Location Manager	Brett Wilson		Effects Editor	Darren Banks
Asst. Location Manager	Joseph Cairns		Re-Recording Mixer	James Feltham
Location Assistant	Georgie Turnbull		Titles	Why Not Associates
Camera Operator	Nick Beek-Sanders		Publicity	Premier PR
Focus Puller	Steve Smith		Music Advisors	Blind Beggar Ltd.
Clapper Loader	Kim Tunstall		BBC Production Exec	Julie Scott
Camera Assistant	Danny Mendieta		Script Editor	Gabriel Silver
Grip	Robin Stone		Sound Recordist	Dave Sansom
Boom Operator	Paul Watson		Make-up & Hair Designer	Emma White
Sound Assistant	Anthony Hurst		Costume Designer	Emma Rosenthal
Gaffer	Brian Jones		Casting Director	David Shaw
Best Boy	Terry Eden		Production Designer	Matthew Gant
Electrician	Danny Griffiths		Music By	Edmund Butt
	Vinny Cowper		Editor	Jeremy Stachan
Genny Operator	Tony O'Brien		Director of Photography	Balazs Bolygo
Art Director	Tom Still		Co-Producer	Marcus Wilson
Standby Art Director	Dan Taylor		Executive Producers	Jane Featherstone
Art Dept Assistant	Andy Hare			Claire Parker
Production Buyer	Ron Pritchard			Matthew Graham
Props Master	Peter O'Rourke			
Prop Hands	Jim Mate			
	Marcus Holt			
Standby Props	Gary Leech			
	Neil O'Rourke			
Standby Carpenter	Gary McCabe			

NORT
DIST

CASE FILE

SERIES TWO
EPISODE FIVE

Co-Created By
Matthew Graham
Tony Jordan
Ashley Pharoah

WRITTEN BY MATTHEW GRAHAM
PRODUCED BY CAMERON ROACH
DIRECTED BY ANDREW GUNN

DCI GENE HUNT	PHILIP GLENISTER
DI SAM TYLER	JOHN SIMM
DS RAY CARLING	DEAN ANDREWS
DC CHRIS SKELTON	MARSHALL LANCASTER
WDC ANNIE CARTWRIGHT	LIZ WHITE
WPC PHYLLIS DOBBS	NOREEN KERSHAW

Sam is suffering from an overdose in the future, making the world of 1973 even more confusing than ever. Simon Lamb's wife and daughter have been kidnapped and are being held hostage against the release of a young man convicted by Hunt a year ago.

In his addled state, Sam must piece together the facts from the old case and find the hostages before it's too late.

MUSIC

You Shouldn't Do That - Hawkwind

Just Like You - Roxy Music

10538 Overture - ELO

Original Broadcast Stats
Run Time: 58' 42"
Transmission: Tuesday 20th March 2007,
              9pm BBC ONE

Viewing Figures for original broadcast:
Overnight Ratings:
Adjusted Ratings: 6.0 million
Audience Share: 6.4 million
                                  26.4%

Adjusted figures include ~~~~~~~~~~~~~~ ~ngs.

Radio Script

My name is Simon Lamb and I wanted this opportunit[y]
talk to the man who has kidnapped my wife and daug[hter]
(emphasise) Bea and Stella because I know in my hea[rt]
you are good man and only want to do the right th[ing]
(pause here)

You have your reasons for the actions you have ta[ken]
You are not a criminal.
(pause here)

You took Bea and Stella to make sure that the ri[ght]
thing is done. You will not hurt them.
(pause here)

You will not harm them in any way because tha[t's]
who you are. You are a good man.
(pause here)

You want justice because you believe an inno[cent]
in prison.

My wife and daughter (pause) Bea and Stella [are]
innocent too and they are imprisoned by yo[u]
that you can see the wrong in that.

[...] the just thing

INT. POTTING SHED - DAY 5/2
BEA and STELLA LAMB are tied up. ANNIE is
trying to reason with DON WITHAM.

ANNIE
You've just gone over it and over it
your mind

DON WITHAM
My Charley worshipped him. He had
power over her and he abused that
power.
BEA LAMB is desperately trying to protest
angrily through her gag

ANNIE
Yes. And she left with Graham.

DON WITHAM
That boy was too simple... He...
(Indicates photo of Lamb)
I've watched him! I... I... I...

ANNIE
No Don...

DON WITHAM
You're not a parent! A parent knows!
The way he looks at them...

ANNIE
No Don. You blame Simon because he
was the last person to see Charley
alive. You blame him because he
could have stopped her dying. He
could've offered to run her home...

DON WITHAM
You're twisting it...

ANNIE
No. You're doing that Don. Twisting
this to blame Simon because really
you want to blame yourself. But
you... Simon... no one could have
known. No one could have stopped
Charley dying.
DON's fury gives way to profound
melancholy.

SIMON LAMB	REECE DINSDALE
MRS BATHURST	LESLEY CLARE O'NEILL
MAVIS WITHAM	OLWEN MAY
DON WITHAM	JONTY STEPHENS
GRAHAM BATHURST	ADAM BERESFORD
MITCH BATHURST	JAMES PETER WELLS
STELLA LAMB	HAYLEY McGROARTY
SCHOOL GIRL 1	ALICIA HALL
SCHOOL GIRL 2	JODIE HAMBLETT

Simon Lamb
(AKA Reece Dinsdale)

Previous Form:
The Chase
Spooks
Home to Roost
A Private Function
Threads

Stunt Co-ordinator	Peter Brayham
1st Assistant Director	Nicki Ballantyne
2nd Assistant Director	Andi Coldwell
3rd Assistant Director	Chantelle Stoffel
Floor Runner	Jack Casey
Production Co-ordinator	Tracy Lee Sapple
Assistant Co-ordinator	Samantha Milnes
Production Office Runner	Danielle Eglin
Continuity	Angie Pontefract
	Steve Walker
Police Advisor	Steve Crimmins
Production Accountant	Diane Pontefract
Assistant Accountant	Matthew Pope
Location Manager	Luc Webster
Asst. Location Manager	Joseph Cairns
Location Assistant	Georgie Turnbull
Camera Operator	Nick Beek-Sanders
Focus Puller	Steve Smith
Clapper Loader	Kim Tunstall
Camera Assistant	Danny Mendieta
Grip	Robin Stone
Boom Operator	Paul Watson
Sound Assistant	Anthony Hurst
Gaffer	Brian Jones
Best Boy	Terry Eden
Electrician	Danny Griffiths
	Vinny Cowper
Genny Operator	Tony O'Brien
Art Director	Tom Still
Standby Art Director	Dan Taylor
Art Dept Assistant	Andy Hare
Production Buyer	Ron Pritchard
Props Master	Peter O'Rourke
Prop Hands	Jim Mate
	Marcus Holt
Standby Props	Gary Leech
	Neil O'Rourke
Standby Carpenter	Gary McCabe
Construction Manager	Chris Watson

Costume Supervisor	Becky Davies
Costume Assistant	Alison Cook
	Amanda Crossley
Make-up Supervisor	Debbie Salmon
Make-up Artist	Amanda Isaacs
Make-Up Assistant	Jenny Ward
Post Prod. Supervisor	Jessica Rundle
Assistant Editor	Penny Clark
Online Editors	Scott Hinchcliffe
	James Osborne
Colourist	Jet Omoshebi
Dialogue Editor	Alex Sawyer
Effects Editor	Darren Banks
Re-Recording Mixer	James Feltham
Titles	Why Not Associates
Animation Sequence	Hot Animation
Publicity	Premier PR
Music Advisors	Blind Beggar Ltd
BBC Production Exec	Julie Scott
Script Editor	Gabriel Silver
Sound Recordist	Dave Sansom
Make-up & Hair Designer	Emma White
Costume Designer	Emma Rosenthal
Casting Director	David Shaw
Production Designer	Matthew Gant
Music By	Edmund Butt
Editor	Liana del Giudice
Director of Photography	Balazs Bolygo
Co-Producer	Marcus Wilson
Executive Producers	Jane Featherstone
	Claire Parker
	Matthew Graham

WEST
T C.I.D.

Co-Created By
Matthew Graham
Tony Jordan
Ashley Pharoah

CASE FILE

SERIES TWO
EPISODE SIX

WRITTEN BY GUY JENKIN
PRODUCED BY CAMERON ROACH
DIRECTED BY ANDREW GUNN

DCI GENE HUNT	PHILIP GLENISTER
DI SAM TYLER	JOHN SIMM
DS RAY CARLING	DEAN ANDREWS
DC CHRIS SKELTON	MARSHALL LANCASTER
WDC ANNIE CARTWRIGHT	LIZ WHITE
WPC PHYLLIS DOBBS	NOREEN KERSHAW

Heroin has hit the streets of Manchester and a Ugandan Asian man is implicated when his brother is found shot.

Sam is haunted by messages from his girlfriend in the future, Maya, as he tries to find out how the drug is being smuggled.

As if that weren't difficult enough, Gene is even more ruthless than normal in his determination to rid the streets of the dealers and Sam must try and ensure justice — rather than vigilantism — is carried out.

MUSIC

Dance With The Devil - Cozy Powell
Breathless - Atomic Rooster
Snow Flower - Ananda Shankar
Rocket Man - Elton John
I Had A Dream - Audience
Hot Sand - Shocking Blue
Traveller In Time - Uriah Heep
Whiskey In The Jar - Thin Lizzy

ELTON JOHN
MCA RECORDS 1972
"ROCKET MAN"
(JOHN/TAUPIN)
MCA RECORDS 1972

INT. RECORD SHOP – DAY – 6/1 – 0826

SAM and GENE run through the shop and into a small chaotic office, past a couple of UNIFORMED PCs. In it, amidst piles of crates, RAY stands over the body of an Asian man of about 30 (DIPAK). GENE, SAM, ANNIE and CHRIS join him. (GENE's rolling breakfast continues. He's onto his bacon and egg sandwich now.)

                    CHRIS
    I wonder what killed him?
                    GENE
    That'd be the bloody enormous hole in
    his chest where the bullet went in.
                    RAY
    When I got here another one of them
    (HE GESTURES AT THE BODY) went
    running out the back, but I couldn't
    catch him.

                    SAM
    Get a description?
                    RAY
    Yeah, I told you ... he was a Paki
    (SAM GIVES HIM A LOOK) Come on, they
    all ...
SAM confronts RAY.

                    SAM
    ... look the same?
SAM looks at RAY with contempt.
                    GENE (to Chris)
    Check the place out. Make sure no-one
    else is here.
RAY's been going through his pockets.
                    RAY
    Here we go... drugs, no surprise
    there...
In the dead man's pockets he's found a lot
of small wraps of drugs. ANNIE's bending
over him and has noticed something.
                    ANNIE
    Boss, there's a viscous yellow liquid
    on his ear.
                    GENE
    That's a drip from my fried egg
    buttie, love. But well done, Miss
    Marple ... that's why we need women
    detectives.

H WEST CITY HOSPITAL

Original Broadcast Stats
Run Time: 57' 29"
Transmission: Tuesday 27th March 2007,
                9pm BBC ONE

Viewing Figures for original broadcast:
    Ratings:
    Audience Share: 62 million
                                    26.5%

Adjusted figures include time-shift recordings.

Ravi   DOB: 22-04-1948 Ugandan-Asian. DNR.
... wound to right clavicle. Comatose on arrival.
... drip to maintain daily balance of nutrients.
...79 - progress as expected. Continue monitoring
... visits and communication reccomended.
... prove no cranial damage.
...85 - Blood pressure now stable at 110/80
...89 - Wound now healing. Toxicology reveals no
... toxins in system. Paracetamol, amoxycillin
... other medical records available (see patient's origin...

MAYA	ARCHIE PANJABI
LAYLA	ALEX REID
ROCKET	TIM PLESTER
RANI	PAUL SHARMA
TOOLBOX TERRY	IAN PULESTON DAVIES
BIG BIRD	LORRAINE CHESHIRE
SKINHEAD	PAUL OLDHAM

Toolbox Terry
(AKA Ian Puleston Davies)

Previous Form:
Vincent
Hustle
Funland
The Bill

Stunt Co-ordinator	Peter Brayham
Stunt Performer	Stewart James
1st Assistant Director	Nicki Ballantyne
2nd Assistant Director	Andi Coldwell
3rd Assistant Director	Chantelle Stoffel
Floor Runner	Jack Casey
Production Co-ordinator	Tracy Lee Sapple
Assistant Co-ordinator	Samantha Milnes
Production Office Runner	Danielle Eglin
Continuity	Angie Pontefract
	Steve Walker
Police Advisor	Steve Crimmins
Production Accountant	Diane Pontefract
Assistant Accountant	Matthew Pope
Location Manager	Luc Webster
Asst. Location Manager	Joseph Cairns
Location Assistant	Georgie Turnbull
Camera Operator	Nick Beek-Sanders
Focus Puller	Steve Smith
Clapper Loader	Kim Tunstall
Camera Assistant	Danny Mendieta
Grip	Robin Stone
Boom Operator	Paul Watson
Sound Assistant	Anthony Hurst
Gaffer	Brian Jones
Best Boy	Terry Eden
Electrician	Danny Griffiths
	Vinny Cowper
Genny Operator	Tony O'Brien
Art Director	Tom Still
Standby Art Director	Andy Hare
Art Dept Assistant	Andy Watson
Production Buyer	Ron Pritchard
Props Master	Peter O'Rourke
Prop Hands	Jim Mate
	Marcus Holt
Standby Props	Gary Leech
	Neil O'Rourke
Standby Carpenter	Gary McCabe

Construction Manager	Chris Watson
Costume Supervisor	Becky Davies
Costume Assistant	Alison Cook
	Amanda Crossley
Make-up Supervisor	Debbie Salmon
Make-up Artist	Amanda Isaacs
Make-Up Assistant	Jenny Ward
Post Prod. Supervisor	Jessica Rundle
Assistant Editor	Penny Clark
Online Editors	Scott Hinchcliffe
	James Osborne
Colourist	Jet Omoshebi
Dialogue Editor	Alex Sawyer
Effects Editor	Darren Banks
Re-Recording Mixer	James Feltham
Titles	Why Not Associates
Publicity	Premier PR
Music Advisors	Blind Beggar Ltd.
BBC Production Exec	Julie Scott
Script Editor	Gabriel Silver
Sound Recordist	Dave Sansom
Make-up & Hair Designer	Emma White
Costume Designer	Emma Rosenthal
Casting Director	David Shaw
Production Designer	Matthew Gant
Music By	Edmund Butt
Editor	Liana Del Giudice
Director of Photography	Balazs Bolygo
Co-Producer	Marcus Wilson
Executive Producers	Jane Featherstone
	Claire Parker
	Matthew Graham

Viewing figures and audience data supplied by David Graham & Associates and BARB/Attentional

NORTH WEST DISTRICT C.I.D

Co-Created By
Matthew Graham
Tony Jordan
Ashley Pharoah

CASE FILE

Series Two
Episode Seven

Written By Mark Greig
Produced By Cameron Roach
Directed By Sj Clarkson

DCI Gene Hunt	Philip Glenister
DI Sam Tyler	John Simm
DS Ray Carling	Dean Andrews
DC Chris Skelton	Marshall Lancaster
WDC Annie Cartwright	Liz White
WPC Phyllis Dobbs	Noreen Kershaw

Filed by DCI Frank Morgan - 20/07/73

TERRY H

DAVI
MACKA
TR. PETE WIL

JULY

MACKAY'S FINAL FIGHT!

Case Summary

"I appear to have killed someone."

Strung out and drunk, Gene Hunt wakes to find himself in the same room as a dead body. That's bad enough, but when all the evidence points to him having been responsible for the killing, his day gets worse. Will Sam be able to prove Gene's innocence? Or will Gene's replacement, the modern-thinking DCI Frank Morgan from Hyde, succeed in building a case against him?

HALL
NG
9PM

NORTH WEST DISTRICT C.I.D

OFFICER REPORT

Officer: DCI Frank Morgan

Activity:

Since arriving at A Division I was struck by the need for not only organisation but a firm hand at the top of the ranking ladder. While I have heard a good deal about many of Gene Hunt's "successes", I can only say that I remain dubious of their validity.

To me there can be no success without order and a clear adherence to the law. For fifteen years this attitude has held me in good stead and yet it would seem such devotion to the legal structure and the security it brings is alien to those in A Division, who deem "close enough" to be the order of the day. It is some relief that the blame must lie with the role model set by DCI Hunt, a man who is to policing and law what a sledgehammer is to Wedgewood china. Still one must cautiously wonder whether the damage to their policing attitude is too ingrained. Would it even be possible to turn this division into the sort of keen and incisive team that modern policing requires? I feel that at this stage it's too early to tell. I will continue to make notes, observe their practice and draw conclusions.

Ultimately this division will come into line with the practices and policies of modern policing. I only hope I am the one to engineer it.

Signed: Frank Morg

Report filed on: 20/07/19

Original Broadcast Statistics

Run Time: 58' 24"
Transmission: Tuesday 3rd April
                   2007, 9pm BBC ONE

Viewing Figures:
Overnight Ratings: 6 million
Adjusted Ratings: 6.4 million
Audience Share: 25.4%

Music

Many A Mile To Freedom - Traffic
Evening Blue - Traffic
Virginia Plain - Roxy Music
Cindy Incidentally - The Faces
Done Me Wrong Alright - Sweet
Cross Roads - Cream
Rock 'n' Roll Disgrace - Sweet
One Of The Boys - Mott The Hoople

NELSON	TONY MARSHALL
FRANK MORGAN	RALPH BROWN
BARRISTER	CORRINNE WICKS
DAVE MACKAY	KIERAN O'BRIEN
TERRY HASLAM	SEAMUS O'NEILL
COLIN MERRICK	JASON WATKINS
PETE WILKES	IAN HANMORE
METER MAN	JOHNNY LEEZE
SUE	GENEVIEVE WALSH

Frank Morgan
(AKA Ralph Brown)

Previous Form:
Spooks
Nighty Night
Star Wars: Episode 1
The Last Train
The Crying Game
Alien³
Withnail and I

Stunt Co-ordinators	Ray Nicholas
	Crispin Layfield
	Vince Keane
Stunt Performers	Brian (Sonny) Nichols
	Mike Lambert
1st Assistant Director	Sam Morris
2nd Assistant Director	Andi Coldwell
3rd Assistant Director	Chantelle Stoffel
Floor Runner	Jack Casey
Production Co-ordinator	Tracy Lee Sapple
Assistant Co-ordinator	Samantha Milnes
Production Office Runner	Danielle Eglin
Continuity	Angie Pontefract
	Steve Walker
Police Advisor	Steve Crimmins
Production Accountant	Diane Pontefract
Assistant Accountant	Matthew Pope
Location Manager	Luc Webster
Asst. Location Manager	Joseph Cairns
Location Assistant	Georgie Turnbull
Camera Operator	Mark Smeaton
Focus Puller	Joe Blackwell
Clapper Loader	Kim Tunstall
Camera Assistant	Danny Mendieta
Grip	Alex Coverley
Boom Operator	Paul Watson
Sound Assistant	Anthony Hurst
Gaffer	Brian Jones
Best Boy	Terry Eden
Electricians	Danny Griffiths
	Vinny Cowper
Genny Operator	Tony O'Brien
Art Director	Tom Still
Standby Art Director	Andy Hare
Art Dept Assistant	Andy Watson
Production Buyer	Ron Pritchard
Props Master	Peter O'Rourke
Prop Hands	Paula Barrington
	David Flower

Standby Props	Neil Glynn
	Neil O'Rourke
Standby Carpenter	Gary McCabe
Construction Manager	Chris Watson
Costume Supervisor	Becky Davies
Costume Assistant	Alison Cook
	Amanda Crossley
Make-up Supervisor	Suzanne Bennett
Make-up Artist	Amanda Isaacs
Make-Up Assistant	Jenny Ward
Post Prod. Supervisor	Jessica Rundle
Assistant Editor	Al Morrow
Online Editors	Scott Hinchcliffe
	James Osborne
Colourist	Jet Omoshebi
Dialogue Editor	Alex Sawyer
Effects Editor	Darren Banks
Re-Recording Mixer	James Feltham
Titles	Why Not Associates
Publicity	Premier PR
Music Advisors	Blind Beggar Ltd.
BBC Production Exec	Julie Scott
Script Editor	Gabriel Silver
Sound Recordist	Dave Sansom
Make-up & Hair Designer	Emma White
Costume Designer	Emma Rosenthal
Casting Director	David Shaw
Production Designer	Matthew Gant
Music By	Edmund Butt
Editor	John Gow
Director of Photography	Tim Palmer
Co-Producer	Marcus Wilson
Executive Producers	Jane Featherstone
	Claire Parker
	Matthew Graham

NORTH WEST DISTRICT C.I.D

Co-Created By
Matthew Graham
Tony Jordan
Ashley Pharoah

CASE FILE

Series Two
Episode Eight

Written By Matthew Graham
Produced By Cameron Roach
Directed By Sj Clarkson

DCI Gene Hunt	Philip Glenister
DI Sam Tyler	John Simm
DS Ray Carling	Dean Andrews
DC Chris Skelton	Marshall Lancaster
WDC Annie Cartwright	Liz White
WPC Phyllis Dobbs	Noreen Kershaw

Filed by DCI Frank Morgan - 27/07/73

M.A.R.S.

METROPOLITAN
ACCOUNTABILITY_AN
RECONCILIATION
STRATEGY

EVIDENCE:
ARTICLE_2611

EVI
AR

EVIDENCE:
ARTICLE_2612

Case Summary

Notorious blagger and cop killer Leslie
Johns is planning a heist on the train
carrying colliery wages. Gene is
determined to infiltrate the criminals and
put Johns behind bars.

Sam has been told by Morgan that his
mission has always been to go undercover
in the department and prove Gene guilty
of negligence.

If he does that he can go home.
With the stakes high and Sam uncertain
in whom to place his trust, he must make
his choice: the future or the past? His
friends or reality?

RHT - NORTH WEST CITY HOSPITAL

Patient
SAM TYLER

OTR Identification
FLLW-TH-YLLW-BRK-RD

Ward
HYDE 2612

Surgeon General
MR FRANK MORGAN

The patient shows repeated signs of mental acuity (despite contrary opinion). A thorough examination of his medical history shows a frequent and steady shift in his response to external stimuli – both auditory and physical – I must wonder then why Sam Tyler has been allowed to simply vegetate when an increase in the stimuli may well have seen a tangible upswing in his condition. Without wishing to overstate the situation, a consistent programme of mental activity (and a steady dose of Fyxic-N or possibly Henisonal) may have seen this poor man up and about earlier. At this rate … inexcusable reticence … his brain scanned … steady course of meds … regular doses of Praxis-H … can look to the cause … more to this man's ill … from a head bump

Episode Eight: Statistics

http://www.statistics.lom.com

Original Broadcast Statistics

Run Time:	59' 52"	
Transmission:	Tuesday 10th April 2007 9pm BBC ONE	
Viewing Figures:		
Ratings:	7 million	Adjusted Ratings: 7.4 million
Audience Share:	28.1%	

Episode Eight: Featured Music

http://www.featuredmusic.lom.com

Music

My Coo Ca Choo	by Alvin Stardust
Funeral For A Friend	by Elton John
Decision/Indecision	by Atomic Rooster
I Hope I Don't Fall In Love With You *(score-only version appears on international and DVD releases)*	by Tom Waits
Over The Rainbow	by Israel Kamakawiwo'ole
Life on Mars?	by David Bowie
One of the Boys	by Mott The Hoople
Changes	by David Bowie

RHT - NORTH WEST CITY HOSPITAL

Visiting Schedule History

Frank Morgan	- Ralph Brown
Leslie Johns	- Sean Gilder
Donald Sykes	- Jack Deam
Ruth Tyler	- Judi Jones
Security Clerk	- Philip Lightfoot
Officer 1	- Jaqueline Boatswain
Officer 2	- Mason Phillips
Test Card Girl	- Harriet Rogers
Nelson	- Tony Marshall

Visiting Specialist:

Leslie Johns (Sean Gilder)

Previous Cases:

Doctor Who
Shameless
New Tricks
State of Play
Hornblower
Gangs of New York

Stunt Co-ordinators	Ray Nicholas
	Crispin Layfield
	Vince Keane
	Tom Lucy
Stunt Performers	Dean Forster
	Juliette Cheveley
	Tina Maskell
	Gary Hoptrough
	Tony Lucken
1st Assistant Director	Sam Morris
2nd Assistant Director	Andi Coldwell
3rd Assistant Director	Chantelle Stoffel
Floor Runner	Jack Casey
Production Co-ordinator	Tracy Lee Sapple
Assistant Co-ordinator	Samantha Milnes
Production Office Runner	Danielle Eglin
Continuity	Angie Pontefract
	Steve Walker
Police Advisor	Steve Crimmins
Production Accountant	Diane Pontefract
Assistant Accountant	Matthew Pope
Location Manager	Luc Webster
Asst. Location Manager	Joseph Cairns
Camera Operator	Mark Smeaton
Focus Puller	Joe Blackwell
Clapper Loader	Kim Tunstall
Camera Assistant	Danny Mendieta
Grip	Alex Coverley
Boom Operator	Paul Watson
Sound Assistant	Anthony Hurst
Gaffer	Brian Jones
Best Boy	Terry Eden
Electricians	Danny Griffiths
	Vinny Cowper
Genny Operator	Tony O'Brien
Art Director	Tom Still
Standby Art Director	Andy Hare
Art Dept Assistant	Andy Watson
Production Buyer	Ron Pritchard
Props Master	Peter O'Rourke
Prop Hands	Paula Barrington
	David Flower

Standby Props	Neil Glynn
	Neil O'Rourke
Standby Carpenter	Gary McCabe
Construction Manager	Chris Watson
Costume Supervisor	Becky Davies
Costume Assistant	Alison Cook
	Amanda Crossley
Make-up Supervisor	Suzanne Bennett
Make-up Artist	Amanda Isaacs
Make-Up Assistant	Jenny Ward
Post Prod. Supervisor	Jessica Rundle
Assistant Editor	Al Morrow
Online Editors	Scott Hinchcliffe
	James Osborne
Colourist	Jet Omoshebi
Dialogue Editor	Alex Sawyer
Effects Editor	Darren Banks
Re-Recording Mixer	James Feltham
Titles	Why Not Associates
Visual Effects Supervisor	Matt Wood
Publicity	Premier PR
Music Advisors	Blind Beggar Ltd.
BBC Production Exec	Julie Scott
Script Editor	Gabriel Silver
Sound Recordist	Dave Sansom
Make-up & Hair Designer	Emma White
Costume Designer	Emma Rosenthal
Casting Director	David Shaw
Production Designer	Matthew Gant
Music By	Edmund Butt
Editor	John Gow
Director of Photography	Tim Palmer
Co-Producer	Marcus Wilson
Executive Producers	Jane Featherstone
	Claire Parker
	Matthew Graham

Patient: Tyler, Sam

HYDE 2612

Well, well, well. Who have you been diddling to get one of these
that or you were very good in a past life. What am I talking abo
Only an exclusive invitation to the premiere of Life On Mars – Th
You'll finally get to find out what's been going on in DI Tyler
Was he back in time, in a coma or stark raving bonkers? You'll get to
know before anyone else. And I finally get some peace from all his
whinging.

typical
Offensive remark

Get yourself to BAFTA, 195 Piccadilly, London, W1 on Wednesday April
4th. Drinks from 7pm, screening from 7.30 pm sharp.

There's no dress code, but try and make an effort eh? The place will be
packed with birds, so unless you're a Catholic priest you might want to
try and impress them. And ladies, if I can't persuade the wife not to
come, I doubt whether I will be attending so don't get your hopes up. But
just in case I do make an appearance, you might like to wear something
red and low cut? (And for God's sake shave your legs, all that feminism
malarkey won't wash with me.)

Sexual harassment

Cheese and wine will be provided, so there's no need to bring a bottle.
Though if you do decide to smuggle in a couple of Blue Nuns or a Mateus
Rosé, I'm sure the lads from the station will turn a blind eye on this
occasion.

on the take

Right that's about it.

Sincerely

C. Hunt

DCI Gene Hunt

Please RSVP by emailing rsvp@kudosfilmandtv.com

Hope you can make it I promise I'll keep him on a lead
DI Sam Tyler

FUNK TO FUNKY...
Afterword by Ashley Pharoah

It started – as most good things do – in a bar. In this case, the bar at BBC Elstree in the early 1990s. It was here that Tony Jordan, Matthew Graham and I first met as writers on *Eastenders* and forged lasting friendships. Although very different writers in many ways, we shared a love of story-telling and an affection for that oft-neglected wing of British film and television which offered an alternative to the dominant discourse of social realism. Or, to put it crudely, we'd rather watch *The Prisoner* than *Cathy Come Home*. So when the independent production company Kudos sent us off on that now notorious trip to Blackpool, it's not surprising that the ideas we came up with reflected a certain longing to move away from the staid and the conventional. We didn't know it then but we'd taken the first steps on what turned out to be a long and remarkable journey.

When Matthew wrote his first drafts of episode one of *Life On Mars* it was into a professional atmosphere of suspicion about 'high concept' television series. 'A contemporary copper waking up in 1973? Wouldn't that work better as a movie? Or a novel? Or a postcard? Or … could you please shut the door on the way out?' What seemed a screamingly obvious good idea to us seemed to just about everyone else to be a little, well, 'silly', to quote a senior executive.

This was a time before *Lost*, *Six Feet Under*, *Heroes*, the new *Doctor Who* and myriad other series proved through ratings and critical success that there are ways of telling stories that don't involve kitchen sinks or people shouting at each other in Liverpool. Every decent journey has obstacles and dark days and we had our fair share, times when we thought about giving up. But whenever Matt and Tony and I

met up, despite how busy we might have been with our other work, we always talked about *Life On Mars*. It fizzed our imaginations. It made us laugh. All we had to do was find people in positions of power who shared our passion and who weren't afraid of going against the social-realist ('Are you absolutely sure you couldn't have some unemployed miners in it?') grain.

We finally found them at the BBC. Matthew's first episode and the concept as a whole had been vigorously interrogated for some seven years by now and sparkled like a diamond, bright and brilliant. But through the making of series one, from the casting and shooting to the editing and music, our loud enthusiasm started to be replaced by some rather subdued doubt. Someone had finally put their money where our mouth was and we looked at the rushes coming down from Manchester and thought 'what on earth are we making?' We didn't have those comforts of genre. We were making a 1970s show set in a coma patient's head and we were nervous. Very, very nervous.

In retrospect that doubt seems preposterous. But how was I to know that we were about to witness one of those rare collisions of talent and timing that happen every now and then? A generation of executives were now in power and they were as hungry as we were to try something new, to push the envelope a little. The production company, Kudos, with the amazing Jane Featherstone driving us on, had proved that high-concept shows like *Hustle* and *Spooks* could find an audience on a mainstream channel. As writers we had honed our craft for many years on more conventional drama series and we were desperate to fly; the lead director, Bharat Nalluri, brought confidence, imagination and a tremendous belief in the

material; the producer, Claire Parker, simply shouldn't have been as good as she was; and the actors, especially John Simm and Philip Glenister, were in some ways just like us writers, experienced and well-regarded but ready to really put their mark on this work, to really let rip.

The idea itself seemed to have found its time, too. The audience didn't worry about whether the idea was 'silly', or in some way not serious and therefore not proper drama. They loved it from the start, in the way a parched garden loves a sparkling tap. They wanted something new and fresh, they wanted to see their 'old' lives of 1973 seen through the ironic prism of 2006. The ratings were good, the critics fulsome, and *Life On Mars* was finally born.

What none of us expected was how *Life On Mars* would suddenly start popping up all over British culture, from newspaper editorials and politicians extolling Gene Hunt's 'instinctive' policing ('Matthew, tell them it was irony.' 'No, no. You tell them.') to *Life On Mars* parties at Scotland Yard (I'm sure they were ironic. Positive.) and from sports commentators comparing the overpaid sportsmen of today with the great heroes of yesteryear to students cleaning the charity shops out of 1970s clothes. Everybody wanted to talk about *Life On Mars*: journalists and critics; friends and family; wonderful websites with loyal, imaginative fans; taxi drivers, of course ('That Gene Hunt, he'd sort out all those Johnny Foreigners flooding in'); school kids who had no idea 1973 was so cool and a lot of older people who knew it wasn't but enjoyed being reminded anyway. It was an astonishing response and I will never forget it.

The last of the pickled eggs has been eaten now. The Cortina has been flogged on eBay. The Party Seven is gathering dust in a props store. That wonderful collision of people and humour that was *Life On Mars* is over. We will all move on, of course, and hopefully produce work that is at least as good. But I suspect that these were the days of our lives, a strange moment in time when idea and audience and actor and writer met in a delicious vortex. For all of you who came on this journey with us and made it so special … thank you so much.

But soft, what sound from yonder cutting-room window bleeds? It's David Bowie again, this time singing 'Ashes to Ashes'. And isn't that Gene Hunt, speeding through London in an Audi Quattro? Surely that can't be Chris in The Blitz Club, wearing a little too much eye-liner? Or Ray's undercover moustache quivering with indignation in a gay club? And that woman there, the one with 'Property Of The Metropolitan Police' stamped on her buttocks? Who is she and why is Gene Hunt looking at her?

I feel another journey starting.

So farewell, *Life On Mars*; farewell, 1973.

See you all in 1981.

Ashley Pharoah
September 2007

Guy Adams (the writer) would like to say:

Life On Mars is a series that inspires devotion. Nonetheless there are four distinct groups who have gone above and beyond in their support of this project.

Firstly: the many members of cast, crew and production staff who have had to tolerate what I generously term 'my sense of humour' both via e-mail and the phone – they all deserve an endless parade of cake, love-slaves and gin for their unfailing helpfulness and positivity. In many ways my inquisition and persistent demands trapped them as securely in 1973 as Sam Tyler.

Secondly: my fellow travellers, Lee, Sally and Nicola who have all worked beyond the call of duty to make these books the best they could be.

Thirdly: the fans and reviewers whose positivity and enthusiasm are sometimes the only fuel a writer's engine needs. I hope this volume delivers all you deserve and expect.

Finally: those who get caught in the crossfire – Ian for picking up my slack when I was too busy with this to fulfil Humdrumming duties, and, of course Debs, Joe, Dan, Mum and Antonio for being forced to talk about little else for months. All writers should be bachelors or orphans – when the work is on they have little room for anything else and bore those around them with their single-minded obsession.

Lee Thompson (the designer) would like to say:

A big thank you to all those who said nice things about the first book; here's hoping this one is just as good! Thanks especially to Keith Topping, who really was very nice indeed.

Buckets of thanks also go out (via courier) to Claire Parker, Cameron Roach, Jane Featherstone and Rebecca at Kudos; to Nikki Ballantyne, Mark Ashmore and Matt Gant from the production team for being such gems on set; to SJ for taking the time and for a really great chat; to Russell, Julie and Phil who are always inspiring; to Claire Potter who has lived side-by-side with the project from day one (and been very forgiving!)

Praise and cries of 'I am not worthy' go out to Nicola for her outstanding (and inimitable) comic art. And for making me not only thinner, but in possession of more hair than my real world counterpart. You are indeed a fabulous person.

And to Sally, extra thanks are sent with bundles of fluffy appreciation for her dedication, her eagle-en-dash eyes and her commitment to both this and the first volume of what has been a labour of love and – above all – a fun journey.

Pocket Books, Guy Adams and Lee Thompson would like to thank the following for providing photographs and for permission to reproduce copyright material. While every effort has been made to trace and acknowledge all copyright holders, we would like to apologise should there have been any errors or omissions.

Except where noted here, all images © Kudos Film and Television.
Photos on pages 52, 53, 54, 55, 56, 57 (except top left and bottom right), 58 (middle row), 59 (bottom four), 60, 61, 62, 63 were supplied by Matt Gant.
Photos on pages 57 (top left and bottom right), 58 (top two), 58 (Bollywood and Peters & Dean scene), 59 (top five), 60 (top two), 78, 79, 80,81 were supplied by Lee Thompson.
Photos on pages 6, 8, 14 were supplied by Claire Parker and Cameron Roach.
Photos on pages 40, 44, 42 were supplied by Tim Palmer.
Photo on page 81 (Mark and the Cortina) was supplied by Mark Ashmore.
Photos on pages 68, 69, 70, 71, 72, 73, 74, 75 were supplied by Hot Animation.
Comic Artwork on pages 122, 123, 124 was drawn and inked by Nicola Bourne. Words by Guy Adams.

Poster (page 11) reproduced with kind permission of the BBC. Based on an original idea created for BBC Marketing by Lee Healy & Amanda Kirke at Red Bee Media, Simon Walter and Nick Bragg at Unreal Design and Brendan Haley at Taylor James.

Original photo of school (page 48, 49) supplied by Sam (aka Samdiablo666, found via flickr.com); Used with permission.
Original photo of Hillman Imp (page 90, 91) supplied by Jules Marshall (aka Mr.M, found via flickr.com); Used with permission.